Daily French Lessons

The New And Proven Concept To Speak French In 36 Days

By

Florence Beaujolie

Table of Contents

Chapter VII: Demonstrative Pronouns And Adjectives 102

Chapter VIII: Common Expressions & Homophones 107

Chapter IX: Negative & Interrogative Forms 115

Answers: 125

Introduction

We're always told that learning a language gets more and more difficult as we grow up, but this is actually not true at all. Adults can sometimes be even better learners than children!

This book is designed especially for adults, or even teenagers, that find it difficult to learn French and understand its rules; it is set up to have easy-to-grasp lessons ranging from two to three and a half pages. They are detail-oriented without being overwhelming, with exercises after each one to help you better understand the rules. Examples are given at each new point of the lesson with precise English translations.

Our book is split into different chapters, with each chapter divided into "days" into a total of 36 days. If you practice for just 20 minutes a day, you will notice a significant improvement in your skills regarding the Language of Love. The lessons get slightly more advanced as the days go by, which is why it is necessary to follow the order they're given in.

We truly believe that our book will help you get the grammar knowledge you were looking for in the simplest of forms, and we hope that you will have fun practicing with it as much as we had fun creating it.

Bon courage!

Chapter I: Pronunciation

Day 1: Letters "S", "C", And "G"

Lesson Reminder:

Letter S:

- If S is at the beginning of a word, it is pronounced as "S". For example: suivre (to follow).
- If S is between two vowels, it is pronounced as "Z". For example: cerise (cherry).
- If S is between a vowel and a consonant, it is pronounced as "S". For example: immense (huge).
- If there is a double S between two vowels, it is pronounced as "S". For example: masser (to massage).

PS: If the letter S is at the end of a word, it is always mute. For example: des livres (books).

Letter C:

- If C is followed by: "a", "o", or "u", it is pronounced as "K". For example: cuisine (kitchen).
- If C is followed by: "i", "e". or an e with a symbol: "é", "è" or "ê", it is pronounced as "S". For example: cent (a hundred).
- If a C is followed by "a", "o", or "u" but it has a cedilla: "ç", it is pronounced as "S". For example: leçon (lesson).

PS: If the letter C is at the end of a word, it is mostly pronounced as "K". For example: lac (lake). But it is also sometimes mute. For example: estomac (stomach).

Letter G:

- If G is followed by: "a", "u", or "o", it is pronounced as "G", like in "go". For example: regarder (to watch).
- If G is followed by: "i", "e", or an e with a symbol, it is pronounced like "J", like in "gender". For example: une gifle (a slap).

- If G is followed by "u", then "i", "e", or an e with a symbol, it is pronounced like "G". For example: une bague (a ring).
- If G is followed by a consonant, it is pronounced like "G". For example: grammaire (grammar).

PS: If the letter G is at the end of a word, it is mute. For example: long (masculine singular for long).

Exercise 1: Give the correct pronunciation for the letter S in these words.

1. Un gosse (a kid): _____
2. Ils lisent (they read): _____
3. Mon estomac (my stomach): _____
4. Le magasin (the store): _____
5. Une fusée (a rocket): _____
6. Tu essaies (you try): _____ / _____
7. Un sosie (a doppelganger): _____ / _____

Exercise 2: Give the correct pronunciation for the letter C in these words.

1. Du sucre (some sugar): _____

2. Le lycée (high school): _____

3. Un garçon (a boy): _____

4. Un cri (a scream): _____

5. Cette (this, in feminine form): _____

6. Convaincre (to convince): _____ / _____

7. Un accident (an accident): _____ / _____

Exercise 3: Give the correct pronunciation for the letter G in the following words.

1. Des griffes (claws): _____

2. Agiter (to shake): _____

3. Je nage (I swim): _____

4. Des algues (algae): _____

5. Un aveugle (a blind person): _____

6. Une gorge (a throat): _____ / _____

7. Un glaçage (icing): _____ / _____

Day 2: Letter E And The Sounds "qu" And "gn"

Lesson Reminder:

Letter E:

- If the letter E is written as a simple "E", it's generally pronounced like the English "ea" from "earn". For example: deviner (to guess).

- But most of the time, it is pronounced like the English "e" from "get". For example: une mouette (a seagull).

- You will get used to differentiate between the two pronunciations with practice. Try to use an audio dictionary to figure it out at first.

- If it is written with symbols on it like "é", "è", or "ê", it is always pronounced like the English "e" from "get". For example: un réveil (an alarm/an alarm clock), ma mère (my mother), un rêve (a dream).

- Their pronunciation is a bit different in terms of the boldness of each one of them, and like in the previous point, it is recommended to use an online tool that would read the words for you in order to get accustomed to them.

PS: If the letter E is at the end of a word, it is always mute. For example: un arbre (a tree).

Sound "qu": The letter Q in French is almost never written alone, just like in English. The only difference is that, in French, it isn't read like the English "qu" from "quick", it is simply read as a "K". For example: un casque (a helmet).

There are only two words in which the letter "Q" isn't followed by "U" and is read as "K": cinq (five) and coq (rooster).

Sound "gn": The combination of those two letters together is pronounced "nye", kind of like how "new" is pronounced, but without making the "u" sound. It just takes the pronunciation of the vowel that comes after it. For example: in le signal (the signal), the "gn" is read as "nya".

Exercise 1: Give the correct pronunciation for the letter E in these words.

1. La fête (the party): _____ / _____
2. Un retour (a return): _____
3. Tu feras (I will [do]): _____
4. Du thé (some tea): _____
5. Un poème (a poem): _____ / _____
6. Une tenue (an outfit): _____ / _____
7. L'église (the church): _____ / _____
8. Devenir (to become): _____ / _____

Exercise 2: Say how the combination of the letters "qu" is pronounced in the following words.

Example: L'équipe (the team): "qu" is pronounced "ki"

1. Une époque (a period of time): "qu" is pronounced _____

2. Des quêtes (quests): "qu" is pronounced _____

3. Quarante (forty): "qu" is pronounced _____

4. Quitter (to leave): "qu" is pronounced _____

5. Le traqueur (the tracker [person]): "qu" is pronounced _____

6. Un cirque (a circus): "qu" is pronounced _____

7. Appel manqué (missed call): "qu" is pronounced

_____

8. Elle taquine (she teases, or she is teasing): "qu" is pronounced _____

Exercise 3: Say how the combination of the letters "gn" is pronounced in the following words.

Example: La dignité (the dignity): "gn" is pronounced "nyi"

1. Ignorer (to ignore): "gn" is pronounced _____

2. La ligne (the line): "gn" is pronounced _____

3. Un témoignage (a testimony): "gn" is pronounced

_____

4. Une bagnole (a car): "gn" is pronounced _____

5. Souligné (highlighted): "gn" is pronounced _____

6. La signification (the meaning): "gn" is pronounced

_____

7. Espagnol (Spanish): "gn" is pronounced _____

8. Ma compagne (my companion, feminine form): "gn" is pronounced _____

Day 3: Sounds

Lesson Reminder:

The Sound "ou": it sounds just like the English "ou" sound from "group". For example: Elle est c<u>ou</u>rte. (She is **short**.)

The Sound "oi": it is pronounced "wa" like in "one". For example: une p<u>oi</u>re (a pear).

The Sound "ui": it is pronounced "wi" like the English "ui" in "quick". For example: une n<u>ui</u>t (a night).

The Sounds "au" And "eau": they are pronounced like the English "o" from "Polly". For example: C'est chaud! (It's hot!); un cad<u>eau</u> (a gift).

The Sounds "eu" And "œu": they are pronounced just like the normal "e" in French. For example: J<u>eu</u>di (Thursday); un c<u>œu</u>r (a heart).

The Sounds "ai", "et", "ei", "er", And "ez": they're all pronounced like the normal French "é". They may slightly vary in depth, so it is recommended to use an online tool that would read the words for you in order to get accustomed to them. For example: du l<u>ai</u>t (some milk); un jou<u>et</u> (a toy); la bal<u>ei</u>ne (the whale); un boulang<u>er</u> (a baker); son n<u>ez</u> (his nose).

The sounds "an, en, on" and "am, em, om": they sound similar to the English "on" from "only". Their pronunciation is a bit different in terms of boldness, so it is recommended to use an online tool that would read the words for you in order to get accustomed to them. For example: bl<u>an</u>c (white); <u>en</u>t<u>en</u>dre (to hear); la m<u>on</u>tre (a wristwatch).

When writing, if the sound "on" comes before the letters "m", "b", or "p", the N must be replaced with M. For example: du jam**b**on (some ham); une tem**p**ête (a storm); le po**m**pier (the firefighter).

Exercise: Write all the previously learned sounds you find in the following words then write how the sound is pronounced in English:

Example: J'ai peur (I'm scared): ai / eu | sounds like: "e" (from get) / "ea" (from "earn").

1. Assez (enough): _____ | sounds like: _____

2. Un bateau (a ship): _____ | sounds like: _____

3. Épuiser (to exhaust): _____ / _____ | sounds like: _____ / _____

4. L'ampoule (the light bulb): _____ /_____ | sounds like: _____ / _____

5. Des nœuds (knots): _____ | sounds like: _____

6. Une fraise (a strawberry): _____ | sounds like: _____

7. Beaucoup (a lot): _____ / _____ | sounds like: _____ / _____

8. Une cuisine (a kitchen): _____ | sounds like: _____

9. L'avion (the airplane): _____ | sounds like: _____

10. Des tiroirs (drawers): _____ | sounds like: _____

11. Le mouton (the sheep): _____ / _____ | sounds like: _____ / _____

12. Seize (sixteen): _____ | sounds like: _____

13. Un œuf (an egg): _____ | sounds like: _____

14. Le carnet (the notebook): _____ | sounds like: _____

Chapter II: Genders, Plurals, And Their Articles

Day 4: Genders

Lesson Reminder:

Here we will be taking a look at feminine and masculine nouns. There are nouns that can be switched from one gender to another. But in this lesson, we will only be reviewing the nouns that take on one specific gender only.

Masculine: you can tell that a noun is masculine if it has one of the following endings:

- **"-ment"**: for example: un bâtiment (a building). Be careful not to confuse these words with adverbs as they almost always end with "-ment", you will get used to them with practice.
- **"-isme"**: for example: un séisme (an earthquake).
- **"-al"**: for example: le journal (the newspaper).
- **"-ier"**: for example: le calendrier (the calendar).
- **"-oir"**: for example: le couloir (the corridor).

– **"-age"**: for example: le fromage (the cheese). Exceptions: la page (the page), la plage (the sea), l'image (the image), la rage (the rage).

Feminine: you can tell that a noun is in feminine if it has one of the following endings:

– **"-ure"**: for example: une voiture (a car).
– **"-té"**: for example: la fidélité (the loyalty).
– **"-ion"**: for example: une option (an option). Exceptions: un lion (a lion).
– **"-ie"** : for example: la pluie (the rain).
– **"-eur"**: for example: la valeur (the value). Exceptions: le bonheur (happiness), le malheur (the misfortune).
– **"-ée"**: for example: une épée (a sword). Exceptions: le lycée (high school), le musée (the museum).
– **"-ance" or "-ence"**: for example: la tendance (the trend), une urgence (an emergency). Exception: le silence (the silence).

PS: Those aren't definite rules for the genders in French. There may be a few more exceptions to each category.

Exercise: Precise the gender of the following nouns: Male (M) or Female (F).

1. Sortie ((the or an exit): ____
2. Carnaval (carnival): ____
3. Quartier (neighborhood): ____
4. Agence (agency): ____
5. Voyage (trip): ____
6. Soir (evening): ____
7. Fumée (smoke): ____
8. Chevelure (hair, or a lock of hair): ____

Day 5: Plurals

Lesson Reminder:

Here we will be taking a look at how to transform a noun from its singular form to its plural form.

In general, a lot of words take an "S" at the end to make them plural just like in English. For example: un cahier (a notebook): des cahiers; une porte (a door): des portes.

Words that end with an S, Z, or X in their singular form don't change at all when in plural forms. For example: un tapis (a carpet): des tapis; un quiz (a quiz): des quiz; une croix (a cross): des croix.

Words that end in "-ou" also take an "S" when turned into their plural form. For example: un cou (a neck): des cous; un bisou (a kiss): des bisous.

There are exceptions to this that take an "X" instead of an "S":

- un bijou (a jewel): des bijoux
- un caillou (a pebble): des cailloux
- un chou (cabbage): des choux
- un genou (a knee): des genoux

- un hibou (an owl): des hiboux
- un pou (a louse): des poux (lice)

Words that end in "-ail" also take "S" when turned into their plural form. For example: un détail (a detail): des details; un épouvantail (a scarecrow): des épouvantails.

Exceptions to this take the ending "-aux":

- le corail (coral): les coraux
- le travail (the job): les travaux
- l'émail (enamel): les émaux
- le vitrail (stained glass): les vitraux
- un soupirail (a basement window): des soupiraux

Words that end in "-al" take on the ending "-aux" when turned into their plural form. For example: spécial (special: spéciaux; natal (native or natal): nataux.

Exceptions to this get an "S" added to the word at the

end: bal (a dance ball), cal (callus), carnaval (carnival), festival (festival), récital (recital), régal (delight).

Words that end with "-eu", "-au", and "-eau" all take an "X" at the end. For example:

- le milieu (the middle or the environment): les milieux
- le noyau (the core): les noyaux
- un couteau (a knife): des couteaux

Exceptions to this get an "S" added at the end: pneu (tire), bleu (blue), landau (pram), and sarrau (smock).

PS: There are words that are irregular and don't follow any rules. For example: un œil (an eye): des yeux; le ciel (the sky): les cieux.

Exercise 1: Turn the following words to their plural form.

1. Oral (oral): _____

2. Joyau (jewel): _____

3. Portail (gate or portal): _____

4. Oiseau (bird): _____

5. Flou (blurred, blurry): _____

6. Nez (nose): _____

7. Canal (channel): _____

8. Concours (contest): _____

Exercise 2: Turn the following words to a singular form.

1. Eaux (waters): _____

2. Rails (tracks, rails): _____

3. Stylos (pens): _____

4. Neveux (nephews): _____

5. Chandails (sweaters): _____

6. Clous (nails, pins): _____

7. Feuilles (papers): _____

8. Manteaux (coats): _____

Day 6: Articles

Lesson Reminder:

"Un" And "Une":

– **Un**: the masculine version of the English "a" or "an", it is placed before non-specific nouns or objects. For example: un atelier (a workshop); un mouchoir (tissue or a handkerchief).

– **Une**: the feminine version of the English "a" or "an", also placed before non-specific nouns and objects. For example: une nuance (a shade); une idée (an idea).

"Le", "La" And "L'...":

– **Le**: the masculine version of the English "the", placed before specific objects and nouns. For example: le cheval (the horse); le lancement (the launching, the start [of a project], or the initiation).

– **La**: the feminine version of the English "the", also place before specific objects and nouns. For example: la gestion (the management); la fierté (the pride).

– **L'...**: This article is also placed before specific objects and nouns, just like "le" and "la". The only difference is that it is gender-neutral, and it is placed before nouns that start with a vowel or an "H". For example: l'allure (the look); l'héroïsme ([the] heroism); l'énergie (the energy); l'usage (the use).

"Les": It is pronounced "lé", it is gender-neutral and is the plural version of "le", "la" and "l'...". It is used before defined objects and nouns just like "the".

"Des": It is pronounced "dé", it is gender-neutral and is the plural version of "un" and "une". It is used before undefined objects and nouns.

Exercise 1: Use the correct gender article before these nouns:

1. _____ cruauté (the cruelty).
2. _____ avancement (an advancement).
3. _____ opinion (the opinion)

4. _____ miroir (the mirror).

5. _____ lueur (a glow).

6. _____ journalisme ((the) journalism).

7. _____ acier ((the) steel).

8. _____ vengeance (a revenge).

Exercise 2: Transform the following nouns into their plural form then put "les" or "des" before each one of them:

1. Un mal (a pain): _____

2. Le pinceau (the paint brush): _____

3. L'épieu (the spear): _____

4. La souris (the mouse): _____

5. Un iglou (an igloo): _____

6. Le camail (the hackle): _____

7. Une voix (a voice): _____

8. L'os (the bone): _____

Day 7: Switching Genders

Lesson Reminder:

In all of the following points, the ending mentioned at first will be replaced with the one following it.

Words that end with "-ier" or "-er" take on the endings "-iére" or "-ère": for example: fier (proud): fière; boulanger (baker): boulangère.

Words that end with "-eur" take on the ending "-euse": for example: fumeur (someone who smokes): fumeuse.

Words that end with "-teur" take on the ending "-trice": for example: acteur (actor): actrice (actress).

PS: Be careful not to confuse the previous three categories with the previously learned invariable words that are only masculine or feminine.

Words that end with "-ien" take on the ending "-ienne": for example: quotidien (daily):

quotidienne.

Words that end with "-if" take on the ending "-ive": for example: pensif (thoughtful): pensive.

Words that end with "-on" take on the ending "-onne": for example: bouffon (jester): bouffonne.

Words that end with "-x" take on the ending "-se": for example: époux (husband): épouse (wife). Except: doux (soft): douce. Be careful not to confuse this category of words with the plural forms of others.

PS: There are words that are irregular and don't follow any rules. For example: un fou (a crazy person): une folle; sec (dry): sèche; un vieux (an old person): une vielle. You will get used to them with practice.

Exercise 1: Transform the following nouns and adjectives from their masculine form to their feminine form.

1. Un prisonnier (a prisoner): Une _____
2. Une jaloux (a jealous person): Une _____
3. Un dépressif (a depressed person): Une _____
4. Un végétarien (a vegetarian person): Une _____
5. Un frimeur (a person who shows off): Une _____
6. Un lion (a lion): Une _____
7. Un passager (a passenger): Une _____
8. Un conducteur (a driver): Une _____

Exercise 2: Transform the following nouns and adjectives from their feminine form to their masculine form.

1. Une politicienne (a politician): Un _____
2. Une rêveuse (a dreamer): Un _____
3. Une sorcière (a witch): Un _____ (a wizard)
4. Une bouchère (a butcher): Une _____
5. Elle est audacieuse (she is bold): Il est _____
6. Une animatrice (a host): Un _____
7. Une sportive (an athletic person): Un _____
8. Une chatonne (a kitten): Un_____

Exercise 3: Indicate the gender of the following words using M or F then transform them into the opposite one.

1. Policier (police officer): _____: _____
2. Spectatrice (spectator): _____: _____
3. Facultatif (optional): _____: _____
4. Chanceux (lucky): _____: _____
5. Espionne (spy): _____: _____
6. Menteur (liar): _____: _____
7. Chère (expensive or dear): _____: _____
8. Logisticienne (logistician): _____: _____

Chapter III: Adjectives And Prepositions

Day 8: Adjectives

Lesson Reminder:

The general rule of adjectives: When using adjectives in French, they have to have the same form as the nouns they are related to. Unlike in English, where the adjective stays the same every time, they change according to the gender of the noun and its quantity (singular or plural).

Examples:

– Masculine singular: un <u>petit</u> garçon (a little boy).
– Feminine singular: une <u>petite</u> fille (a little girl).
– Masculine plural: des <u>petits</u> garçons (little boys).
– Feminine plural: des <u>petites</u> filles (little girls).

Types of adjectives: In French, there are two types of adjectives:

- The first type is called "**adjectif épithète**". It is placed right before or after the noun it qualifies with nothing separating them. For example: un grand mur (a big wall); une feuille blanche (a white paper).

- The second type is called "**adjectif attribut**". It is linked to the noun with the use of a descriptive verb. The verbs that come before "un adjectif attribut" usually are: être (to be), sembler (to seem), paraître (to appear), devenir (to become), rester (to stay), demeurer (to remain), avoir l'air (to look or to look like), passer pour (to pass for).

- For example:
  o Ses yeux **sont** bleus (his/her eyes **are** blue)
  o la chaise **semble** vieille (the chair **seems** old)
  o la valise **a l'air** lourde (the suitcase **looks** heavy)

Exercise 1: Mention the gender "M or F" and the quantity "S or P" of the following adjectives.

1. La soupe est chaude. (The soup is hot.): ____ / ____

2. Le film est trop <u>long</u>. (The movie is too long.): ____ / ____

3. Des stylos <u>verts</u> (green pencils): ____ / ____

4. Ces robes sont <u>chères</u>. (These dresses are expensive.): ____ / ____

5. Une <u>belle</u> écriture (beautiful writing): ____ / ____

6. Des rues <u>lumineuses</u> (bright streets): ____ / ____

7. Le restaurant est <u>ouvert</u>. (The restaurant is open.): ____ / ____

8. Je suis <u>heureux</u>. (I am happy.): ____ / ____

Exercise 2: Transform the following adjectives into the mentioned forms.

1. Gentille (kind) F/S: _____ F/P

2. Douloureux (painful) M/P: _____ F/P

3. Protectrices (protective) F/P:_____ M/S

4. Mauvais (bad) M/S: _____F/P

5. Craintifs (fearful) M/P: _____F/S

6. Dernière (last) F/S: _____M/P

7. Pluvieux (rainy) M/P: _____F/S

8. Légères (light) F/P: _____M/S

Exercise 3: Put "A" for "adjectif attribut" or "E" for "adjectif épithète".

1. Il est <u>adorable</u>. (He is adorable.): ____
2. Un endroit <u>mystérieux</u> (a mysterious place): ____
3. La pièce semble <u>spacieuse</u>. (The room seems spacious.): ____
4. Des réunions <u>importantes</u> (important meetings): ____
5. Tu as l'air <u>anxieuse</u>. (You look anxious.): ____
6. Une réponse <u>fausse</u> (a wrong answer): ____
7. Un voyage <u>fatigant</u> (a tiring trip): ____
8. Les dégâts restent <u>considérables</u>. (The damage stays significant.): ____

Day 9: Prepositions Related To Time 1

Lesson Reminder:

"à" or "au": their literal translation is "at". They're used to indicate the exact hour of an event, before centuries or before the spring season. For example: On se voit **à** 10h. (We'll meet **at** 10 am.); **au** vingtième siècle (**in** the 20th century); **au** printemps (**in** spring).

"de... à..." or "du... au...": their literal translation is "from... to ...". It is used the same way as in English. For example: La réunion est **de** 9h **à** 10h. (The meeting is **from** 9 am **to** 10 am.); L'événement dure **du** Samedi **au** Mercredi. (The event lasts **from** Saturday **to** Wednesday.)

"quand": its literal translation is "when". It is used like in English, to ask questions about time and to indicate an event happening after another. For example: **Quand** est-ce qu'on part ? (**When** are we leaving?); Je t'aiderai **quand** je rentre. (I'll help you **when** I'm back home.)

"après": its literal translation is "after". It is used the same way as in English. For example: Il rentre **après** 20h. (He returns **after** 8 pm.); Le film commence **après** les cours. (The movie starts **after** school.)

"avant": its literal translation is "before". It is used the same way as in English. For example: Il rentre **avant** 20h. (He returns **before** 8 pm.); Je prends une douche **avant** de sortir. (I take a shower **before** going out.)

"dans": its literal translation is "in". It is used the same way as in English. For example: Elle arrive **dans** une heure. (She arrives **in** one hour.)

Exercise: Use the right preposition to fill in the blanks.

1. Ranger ta chambre _____ tu finis. (Cclean up your room when you're done.)
2. Mon vol est _____ 1h 30. (My flight is at 1:30 am.)
3. Tu dois être présent 30 minutes _____ le début. (You have to be present 30 minutes before the start.)

4. Va voir ta tante _____ le dîner. (Go see your aunt after dinner.)

5. Les heures de visite sont _____ 11h _____ 15h. (Visiting hours are from 11 am to 3 pm.)

6. Le train arrive _____ 15 minutes. (The train will arrive in 15 minutes.)

7. J'adore faire des randonnées _____ printemps. (I love hiking in spring.)

8. Elles seront occupées _____ Dimanche _____ Jeudi. (They will be busy from Sunday to Thursday.)

Day 10: Prepositions Related To Time 2

Lesson Reminder:

"depuis": its literal translation is "since". It is used the same way as in English but also in another form. For example:

– **depuis** 1996 (**since** 1996)

– Ils sont là **depuis** 3 heures. (They've been here **for** 3 hours.)

- Il pleut **depuis** que nous sommes sortis. (It's been raining **ever since** we went out.)

"dès" or "dès que..." and "à partir de...": their literal translation is "from", but they're used to say "starting from". For example:

- Tu seras parti **dès** Lundi. (You will be gone **from** Monday **on**.)
- Je serai au bureau **à partir de** 8h. (I'll be at the office **starting from** 8 am.)

"Dès que" is mostly used when something needs to happen, or that has happened immediately after the time frame given, a bit like "as soon as". For example: Appelle moi **dès que** tu arrives. (Call me **as soon as** you get there.) It's one of those expressions that sound more natural in French than when translated.

"en": its literal translation is "in". It is used like in English with months, years and seasons except for spring. For example:

- Le criminel a été arrêté **en** Février. (The criminal was arrested **in** February.)
- Ce bâtiment a été abandonné **en** 1985. (This building was abandoned **in** 1985.)
- La forêt est plus belle **en** automne. (the forest is prettier **in** fall.)

"jusqu'à" or "jusqu'en": their literal translation is "until". It is used the same way as in English, but "jusqu'en" is used before months and years. For example:

- La cérémonie continuera **jusqu'à** 19h. (The ceremony will continue **until** 7 pm.)
- Mon colis n'arrivera que **jusqu'en** Juin. (my package won't arrive **until** June.)

"pendant": its literal translation is "during". It is used to indicate an event happening for a period of time. For example:

- Je serai là **pendant** les vacances. (I'll be here **during** the holidays.)

- Je serai là **pendant** 3 mois. (I'll be here **for** 3 months.)

- Je cuisinerai **pendant** que tu finisses. (I'll cook **while** you finish.)

Exercise: Use the right preposition to fill in the blanks.

1. Le magasin est ouvert _____ 20h. (The store is open until 8 pm.)

2. Tu peux me passer ton cahier _____ la récréation s'il te plaît ? (Could you pass me your notebook during recess, please?)

3. On part à Tokyo _____ été. (We're going to Tokyo in summer.)

4. Ils sont mariés _____ 5 ans. (They've been married for 5 years.)

5. Je commence à travailler _____ Lundi prochain. (I start working starting from next Monday.)

6. La pièce est devenue silencieuse _____ le film a commencé. (The room went silent as soon as the movie started.)

7. Il reste à l'hôpital _____ Décembre. (He'll stay at the hospital until December.)

Day 11: Prepositions Related To Space 1

Lesson Reminder:

"à": its literal translation is "in" or "at". It is used before cities and specific buildings. For example:

- Nous nous sommes rencontrés **à** Paris. (We met **in** Paris.)
- Je révise **à** la bibliothèque. (I'm studying **at** the library.)

"au" or "aux": their literal translation is "in" or "at". Just like the previous one, but they're used before countries that have masculine names. For example:

- Je suis **au** Maroc. (I'm **in** Morocco.)
- Il est **aux** États Unis. (He's **in** the United States.)

"à droite" and "sur la droite de": their literal

translations are "right" and "on the right side of". They're used just like in English. For example:

- Tourner **à droite** (turn **right**)
- **Sur la droite de** mon miroir (**on the right side of** my mirror)

Sometimes "à droite de" is used instead of "sur la droite de", but it's less frequent.

"à gauche" and "sur la gauche de": their literal translations are "left" and "on the left side of". They're used just like in English. For example:

- Tourner **à gauche** (turn **left**)
- **Sur la gauche de** mon miroir (**on the left side of** my mirror)

Sometimes "à gauche de" is used instead of "sur la gauche de", but it's less frequent.

"à côté de" or "à côté du": their literal translation

is "next to", used just like in English. For example:

- Mes clefs sont **à côté de** mon portefeuille. (My keys are **next to** my wallet.)
- La table est **à côté du** canapé. (The table is **next to** the sofa.)

"au-dessus de" and "au-dessous de": their literal translations are "above" and "underneath", respectively. They are used just like in English. For example:

- Nous vivons **au-dessus d'**un restaurant. (We live **above** a restaurant.)
- Mon chat se cache **au-dessous de** la table. (My cat hides **underneath** the table.)

"sur" and "sous": their literal translations are "on" and "under". They're used just like in English. For example:

- Le livre est **sur** mon bureau. (The book is **on** my desk.)

– Mon oreiller est tombé **sous** le lit. (My pillow fell **under** the bed.)

"loin de" and "près de": their literal translations are "near" and "far from". They're used just like in English. For example:

– Mon ami vit **loin de** chez nous. (My friend lives **far from** us.)

– Mon ami vit **près de** chez nous. (My friend lives **near from** us.)

Exercise: Fill in the blanks using the right preposition.

1. Mon hamster était _____ le chapeau. (My hamster was under the hat.)

2. La Statue de la Liberté se trouve _____ New York. (The Statue of Liberty is located in New York.)

3. Le parc est _____ la plage. (The park is close to the beach.)

4. Mon sac est _____ tes affaires. (My purse is next to your stuff.)

5. J'ai une belle veilleuse _____ ma table de nuit. (I have a pretty nightlight above my bedside table.)

6. Il y'a une librairie non _____ De notre école. (There is a library not far from our school.)

7. Il a mis tes clefs _____ le bar. (He put your keys on the bar.)

8. En entrant dans le magasin, tu trouveras le riz _____ la section des pâtes. (When entering the store, you'll find the rice on the left side of the pasta section.)

9. Mon chien aime rester _____ du chauffage durant les journées froides. (My dog likes to stay underneath the heater during cold days.)

Day 12: Prepositions Related To Space 2

Lesson Reminder:

"au-delà de" and "à travers" or "par": their literal translations are "beyond" and "through" or "across" respectively. They're used just like in English. For example: **au-delà des** montagnes (**beyond** the mountains); **à travers** l'océan (**through** the ocean); Je regarde **par** la fenêtre. (I look **through** the window.) When translating, "across" is used to say "par" with roads.

"devant" and "derrière": their literal translations are "in front of" and "behind", respectively. They're used just like in English. For example:

- Il y'a un jardin **devant** notre maison. (There's a garden **in front of** our house.)
- Il y'a un jardin **derrière** notre maison. (There's a garden **behind** our house.)

"dans" and "en": their literal translation is "in", but they're used in different contexts. "Dans" is used before rooms, means of transport, or before books and newspapers. For example:

- Je suis **dans** la salle de bain. (I'm **in** the bathroom.)
- Je suis **dans** le métro. (I'm **in** the metro.)

– J'ai lu ça **dans** le journal. (I read that **in** the newspaper.)

"En" is used before countries that have a feminine name. For example: Je suis **en** France. (I'm **in** France.)

"chez": its literal translation is "at". It is used the same way as in English. For example:

– Je suis **chez** le dentiste. (I'm **at** the dentist's clinic.)
– Je suis **chez** ma copine. (I'm **at** my friend's house.)

"de" or "du": their literal translation is "from". They are used the same way as in English. For example:

– Il rentre **de** France. (He's returning **from** France.)
– Il rentre **du** centre-ville. (He's returning **from** downtown.)

"vers": its literal translation is "towards". It is used the same way as in English. Example: Je marche **vers**

les arbres. (I'm walking **towards** the trees.)

"en dehors de" and "dehors": their translations are "outside of" and "outside", respectively. They're used just like in English. For example:

– Je suis **en dehors de** l'école. (I'm **outside of** the school.)
– Attends moi **dehors**. (Wait for me **outside.**)

"en face de" or "en face du": their literal translation is "facing". It is used the same way as in English. For example: La banque se trouve **en face du** centre commercial. (The bank is located **facing** the mall.)

Exercise: Fill in the blanks using the right preposition.

1. Elle est _____ la coiffeuse. (She's at the hairdresser's salon.)

2. Tu dois passer _____ cette ruelle. (You have to go across this alley.)

3. Nous allons _____ la plage. (We're going towards the beach.)

4. Il y'a une petite boutique de vêtements _____ ce marché. (There's a little clothing shop behind this market.)

5. L'Afrique se trouve _____ la Mer Méditerranée. (Africa is located beyond the Mediterranean Sea.)

6. Il s'est installé _____ Chine. (He settled down in China.)

7. Il y'a une petite exposition d'arts _____ la grande villa. (There is a small art expo facing the big villa.)

8. Les ingrédients sont _____ le troisième tiroir. (The ingredients are in the third drawer.)

9. Ils sont tous _____ la salle de cinéma. (They're all outside of the movie theater.)

10. Le petit garçon marche _____ ses parents. (The little boy is walking in front of his parents.)

11. Nous regardons le film _____ ces lunettes 3D. (We are watching the movie through these 3D glasses.)

Day 13: Important Prepositions

Lesson Reminder:

Important abbreviations to remember:

- **à + le = au**: used before masculine nouns; for example: café au lait (coffee with milk).
- **à + les = aux**: used before plural nouns; for example: une tarte aux fraises (a strawberry pie).
- **de + le = du**: used before masculine nouns; for example: loin du marché (far from the market).
- **de + les = des**: used before plural nouns; for example: à côté des maisons (next to the houses).

It is **very** important to remember these as they are used all the time in the French language. Not just with prepositions, but they also sometimes replace the articles that come before nouns.

"avec" and "sans": their literal translations are "with" and "without". They're used the same way as in English. For example: viens **avec** moi (come **with** me); **avec** plaisir (**with** pleasure); vas y **sans** moi (go **without** me); **sans** regrets (**without** regrets).

"en": its literal translation is "by" when used before means of transportation, but it is also used to describe the material of something, and that doesn't have a translation in English. For example: Je pars **en** voiture. (I'm leaving **by** car.); un pull **en** laine (a wool sweater).

"à" or "au": just like "en", its literal translation is "by" when used before means of transportation, but it is also used to describe an ingredient in a dish or certain machines. For example: Je pars **à** pieds. (I'm leaving **by** foot.); une tarte **au** citron (a lemon pie); une machine **à** café (a coffee machine).

"malgré" and "grâce à": their literal translations are "despite" and "thanks to". They are used the same way as in English. For example: Je sors **malgré** la chaleur. (I'm going out **despite** the heat.); C'est **grâce à** toi. (It's all **thanks to** you.)

"entre": its literal translation is "between". It is used like in English. For example: Ça doit rester **entre** nous. (This has to stay **between** us.)

Exercise: Fill in the blanks with the right preposition.

1. Ils ont besoin de plus de pailles _____ acier. (They need more steel straws.)
2. J'ai mis mon t-shirt dans la machine _____ laver. (I put my shirt in the washing machine.)
3. Le gâteau _____ fruits de ma tante est délicieux. (My aunt's fruit cake is delicious.)
4. Le vieux est sauvé _____ docteur qui était dans les environs. (The old man is saved thanks to the doctor that was around the area.)

5. J'ai vu un petit renard _____ les buissons. (I saw a little fox between the bushes.)

6. Emmenez ton petit frère _____ toi au parc. (Take your little brother with you to the park.)

7. Il fait chaud, ne sortez pas _____ bouteilles d'eau. (It's hot outside, don't go out without water bottles.)

8. _____ ce que tout le monde dit, tu dois continuer à te battre pour tes rêves. (Despite what everyone says, you should keep fighting for your dreams.)

Day 13: Important Prepositions

Lesson Reminder:

"de" or "du": its literal translation is "from" or "by". It is used to describe the origin of something (where it came from), who it belongs to or the creator of something like a book. For example: un livre **de** la bibliothèque (a book **from** the library); le livre **de** Mark (Mark's book); un livre **de** Lauren Kate (a book **by** Lauren Kate).

"pour": its literal translation is "to" or "for". It is used to express a cause, a purpose or a destination, it can also be used to express being okay with something. For example:

- Il a été arrêté **pour** vol. (He was arrested **for** theft.)
- Je fais du sport **pour** maigrir. (I work out **to** get in shape.)
- Ce cadeau est **pour** ma mère. (This gift is **for** my mom.)
- Je suis **pour** cette idée. (I am **for** this idea.)

"contre": its literal translation is "against". It is used the same way as in English. For example: Je suis **contre** cette idée. (I'm **against** this idea.)

PS: It can also be used with space. For example: **contre** le mur (**against** the wall).

"par": its literal translation is "by" or "via". It is used to introduce the means used to do something, the person that made something, or to indicate how many times something needs to be done. For example:

- Je viens **par** bus. (I'm coming **by** bus.)
- Je t'ai envoyé un message **par** email. (I sent you a message **via** email.)
- Deux fois **par** jour (twice **a** day).

"excepté" or "sauf" and "sauf si": their literal translations are "except" but "sauf si" means "unless". They are used just like in English. For example: Tous sont venus **sauf** Paul. (Everyone came **except** Paul.); Ne sors pas **sauf si** tu finis tes devoirs. (Don't go out **unless** you finish your homework.)

PS: "excepté" and "sauf" are interchangeable, but "sauf" is more frequently used.

Exercise: Fill in the blanks with the right preposition.

1. Mon frère a eu une promotion _____ ses efforts. (My brother got a promotion for his efforts.)

2. Elle a aimé toutes les robes _____ la rouge. (She liked all the dresses except the red one.)

3. Son visage est rempli _____ joie. (Her face is full of happiness.)

4. Je suis _____ les résultats du vote. (I am against the voting results.)

5. Je vais faire le tour d'Europe _____ train. (I will tour Europe by train.)

6. Je ne te prendrai pas avec moi que _____ tu me promets de bien te comporter. (I won't take you with me unless you promise to behave.)

Chapter IV: Object Complements And Circumstantial Complements

Day 15: COD And COS

Lesson Reminder:

Object complements point out the person or the thing on which the action is done. Let's see the different types of object complements.

Compléments d'Objets Directes: It translates to Direct Object Complements and they are referred to as "COD". They are directly linked to the verb without any preposition separating them, and they answer the questions, "Qui ?" (who?) and "Quoi ?" (what?). For example:

– J'appelle **ma mère.** (I'm calling **my mom.**) -> J'appelle **qui** ? (**Who** am I calling?) -> **Ma mère (My mother)**.

– Je bois **du thé**. (I'm drinking **some tea.**) -> Je bois **quoi** ? (**What** am I drinking?) -> **Du thé (some tea)**.

PS: The verbs that introduce CODs are called "verbes transitifs directes" (direct transitional verbs), they are all the verbs that **need** a COD to be able to understand the meaning of the sentence. For example, the verb "marcher" (to walk) doesn't need a COD. It is simply put in a sentence "Je marche." (I am walking.) Verbs like these are called "verbes intransitifs" (non-transitional verbs).

Compléments d'Objets Seconds: It translates to Secondary Object Complements, and they are referred to as "COS". They are introduced after a COD with the use of a preposition. They are not necessary to the meaning of the sentence and can be eliminated. They are linked to the same verb as the COD that precedes them. If another verb is introduced, then it can't be considered a COS. For example:

– Je bois du café <u>pour</u> *bien me réveiller.* (I drink coffee <u>to</u> *wake up.*)

PS: The verbs that introduce COSs are also "verbes transitifs directes", just like CODs.

Exercise: Underline the Object Complements in the following sentences and precise their nature (COD/COS).

1. On a fait un cours intéressant aujourd'hui. (We had an interesting class today.): _____

2. J'ai perdu mon chapeau de Noël. (I lost my Christmas hat.): _____

3. Mon père a fait un gâteau pour mon anniversaire. (My father baked a cake for my birthday.): _____

4. Mon cousin a perdu ses lunettes. (My cousin lost his glasses.): _____

5. Je mange mon diner. (I'm having my dinner.): _____

6. Elle entend son chien courir en ouvrant la porte de son appartement. (She hears her dog running while opening her apartment's door.): _____

Day 16: COI

Lesson Reminder:

Compléments d'Objets Indirectes: It translates to Indirect Object Complements, and they are referred to as "COI". They are indirectly linked to the verb via a preposition separating them. They answer the questions "À qui ?/À quoi ?" (Whose?/To or for what?) and "De qui ?/De quoi ?" (From or of who?/From or of what?). For example:

- Cette robe appartient <u>à</u> **Aileen**. (This dress belongs <u>to</u> **Aileen**.) **À qui** appartient cette robe ? (**Whose** dress is this?) -> <u>À</u> **Aileen** (<u>to</u> **Aileen**).
- Il a peur <u>de</u> **tomber**. (He's afraid <u>of</u> **falling**.) -> Il a peur **de quoi** ? (He's afraid **of what**?) -> <u>De</u> **tomber** (<u>of</u> **falling**).

Be careful; the meaning can sometimes be lost in the translation when asking the question. For example:

- Fais confiance <u>à</u> **ton père**. (Trust **your father**.) -> Fais confiance **à qui** ? (Trust **who**?) -> **À ton père** (**your father**).

See how we didn't use the question form given in the translation above? For this reason, it's better not to count on them to know if it's a COI or a COD, the best option would be to learn your prepositions to be able to differentiate them from articles.

PS: The verbs that introduce COIs are called "verbes transitifs indirectes" (indirect transitional verbs). They **need** a COI to be able to understand the meaning of the sentence. One sentence could also contain both a COD and a COI.

Be careful, if the prepositions "à" or "de" come after a verb and introduce a **place** or a **time**, what comes after them is **not a COI**, that verb is still considered "verbe intransitif" or "verbe transitif directe" if it has a COD.

Exercise 1: Underline the Object Complements in the following sentences and precise their nature

(COD/COI).

1. Prends soin de ton petit frère. (Take care of your little brother.): _____

2. Ma mère a adoré le cadeau de papa ! (My mom loved dad's gift!): _____

3. Tu t'intéresses vraiment aux arts. (You're very interested in arts.): _____

4. Elle a besoin du médicament prescript. (She needs the prescribed medicine.): _____

5. Faites attentions aux voitures en traversant la route. (Be careful of the cars when crossing the road.): _____

6. Nous tenons beaucoup à nos chats. (We are really attached to our cats.): _____

Exercise 2: Determine the nature of the verbs in the following sentences, write "VTD" for "verbe transitif directe", "VTI" for "verbe transitif indirecte" or "VI" for "verbe intransitif".

1. Nous allons à la plage. (We're going to the beach.): _____

2. Passe moi le couteau. (Pass me the knife.):

_____

3. Ça dépend du temps. (It depends on the weather.):

_____

4. Ramenez vos serviettes avec vous. (Bring your towels with you.): _____

5. Elle est rentrée de son voyage. (She came back from her trip.): _____

6. Ils habitent à Toronto. (They live in Toronto.):

_____

7. Mettez les chaises au fond. (Put the chairs in the back.): _____

8. Mon père se réveille à 6h. (My father wakes up at 6 am.): _____

9. Tu joues à quoi ? (What are you playing?):

_____

Day 12: Circumstantial Complements

Lesson Reminder:

Circumstantial complements add more meaning and preciseness to the sentence. They can be placed at the beginning or at the end of the sentence. They can usually even be moved around or even deleted, but it's not always the case.

Let's take a look at their different types:

Complément Circonstanciel de Temps: It translates to Circumstantial Complement of Time. They are referred to as CCT. Much like their name suggests, they are an indication of the time in which the verb takes action in. They usually come after a preposition related to time but not all the time. For example: Je reviens à **minuit**. (I'll be back at **midnight**.); **Ce soir**, je reviens un peu tard. (**Tonight** I'll be back a bit late.) They answer the question, "Quand ?" (When?).

Complément Circonstanciel de Lieu: It translates to Circumstantial Complement of Place/Space. They are referred to as CCL. They are an indication of the place in which the verb is taking action. They usually come after a preposition related to space but not all the time. For example: Le chat se cache <u>dans</u> **la boîte**. (The cat hides <u>in</u> **the box**.); Ils sont tous **dehors**. (They're all **outside**.) They answer the question, "Où ?" (Where?).

Complément Circonstanciel de Manière: It translates to Circumstantial Complement of Way/Manner. They are referred to as CCM. They indicate how an action is done. They are sometimes introduced by a preposition and other times. They are an adverb. For example: Elle sourit <u>avec</u> **gentilesse**. (She smiles <u>with</u> **kindness**.); Elle sourit **gentiment**. (She smiles **kindly**.). They answer the question, "Comment ?" (How?).

Exercise: Identify the Circumstantial Complements by underlining them in the following sentences then precise their nature (CCL/CCT/CCM).

1. La maison était très calme ce matin. (The house was so calm this morning.): _____

2. Les enfants jouent bruyamment. (The kids are playing loudly.): _____

3. Nous dînons à table. (We are dining on the table.): _____

4. Elle a géré l'événement avec confiance hier. (She managed the event with confidence yesterday.): _____ / _____

5. Mon mari et moi partons à Las Vegas en été. (My husband and I are going to Las Vegas in the summer.): _____ / _____

6. Il marche devant moi en toute timidité. (He's walking in front of me timidly.): _____ / _____

7. L'autre jour au restaurant, ton frère parlait avec tristesse. (The other day at the restaurant, your brother was talking with sadness.): _____ / _____ / _____

Chapter V: Personal Pronouns

Day 18: Subject Pronouns

Lesson Reminder:

Les Pronoms Sujets: It translates to "subject pronouns". They are the pronouns we use in conjugation and to replace the subject. These pronouns are: "Je" (I), "Tu" (You), "Il/Elle" (He/She/It), "Nous" (We), "Vous" (You, plural form), "Ils/Elles" (They, masculine and feminine form).

There's also the pronoun "On", which means "We", but it is conjugated like "Il/Elle".

Exercise: Put the correct personal pronoun in the blanks.

1. _____ a tout abandonné pour poursuivre sa passion. (He abandoned everything to pursue his passion.)
2. Attention, _____ vas tomber ! (Be careful, you're going to fall!)

3. _____ sont endormies dans le salon. (They [feminine] are asleep in the living room.)

4. _____ pars chez ma grand-mère. (I'm going to grandma's.)

5. _____ enlève ses chaussures avant d'entrer. (She takes her shoes off before going inside.)

6. _____ regardons un film triste. (We're watching a sad movie.)

7. _____ lisez quoi ? (What are you [plural] reading?)

8. _____ chantent trop bien ! (they (masculine) sing very well!).

Day 19: Tonic Pronouns

Lesson Reminder:

Les Pronoms Toniques: It translates to "tonic pronouns". They are usually used after a preposition, to ask a question about someone or to introduce someone: "Moi" (I or Me), "Toi" (You), "Lui/Elle" (He/She), "Nous" (We), "Vous" (You), "Eux/Elles" (They masculine and feminine). For example:

- **Moi**, je suis Français. (I'm French.)
- Il aime le café, **lui** ? (Does he like coffee?)
- Faites comme chez **vous**. (Make yourselves at home.)

Exercise: Put the correct tonic pronoun in the blanks.

1. Je préfère la natation, et _____? (I prefer swimming, and you?)
2. Elles prennent toute la responsabilité sur _____. (They take all the responsibility on them [feminine]).
3. Ton sac est devant _____. (Your bag is in front of me.)
4. _____, elle vient de partir. (She just left.)
5. On passe la nuit chez _____. (We'll spend the night at your [plural] house.)
6. Elle les attend avec _____. (She's waiting for them with him.)
7. J'ai acheté des glaces pour _____ tous. (I bought ice cream for us all.)
8. _____, ils partent en Afrique. (They're going to Africa.)

Day 20: Reflected Pronouns

Lesson Reminder:

Les Pronoms Réfléchis: It translates to "reflected pronouns". They are the pronouns used before the actions that one does on oneself or one does by themselves: "Je me" (myself), "Tu te" (yourself), "Il/Elle se" (himself/ herself), "Nous nous" (ourselves), "Vous vous" (yourselves), "Ils/Elles se" (themselves).

The translation given isn't really used in English. It's only there to understand the pronouns better. For example:

– **Je me** balade. (I'm on a walk.)
– **Tu t'**habilles. (You're getting dressed.)
– **Nous nous** demandons pourquoi il a tardé. (We're wondering why he's late.)

Exercise: Put the correct reflected pronoun in the

blanks.

1. _____ sont absentées. (They [feminine] were absent.)

2. _____ trompes. (You are wrong.)

3. _____ lamente. (He is complaining.)

4. _____ méfie. (I am wary.)

5. _____'entre-tuent. (They [masculine] are killing each other.)

6. _____ rappelons. (We remember.)

7. _____ fie à sa sœur. (She trusts her sister.)

8. _____ souciez trop. (You [plural] are worrying too much.)

Day 21: COD Pronouns

Lesson Reminder:

They're called "pronoms COD", let's take a look at them:

Some of them are used to replace a COD in a paragraph after it's been mentioned once before to avoid repetition: "Le/La/L'..." (It/Him/Her) and "Les"

(Them). To figure out which item of the sentence they refer to, simply ask the questions "Quoi ?" or "Qui ?".

For example:

Je mange <u>la pomme</u> puis je jette **la pomme**. (I eat <u>the apple</u> then I throw **the apple**.)

Je mange <u>la pomme</u> puis je **la** jette. (I eat <u>the apple</u> then I throw **it**.)

Je jette **quoi** ? (**What** do I throw?)

<u>La pomme</u>. (<u>The apple</u>.)

The pronoun "en" also replaces a COD that has been previously mentioned in the sentence to avoid repetition. In this case, "en" usually means "some of it/of it". To figure out the function and which item of the sentence it refers to, simply ask the questions "Quoi ?" or "Qui ?"

For example:

Je vois <u>un gâteau</u> et je prends une part **du gâteau**. (I see <u>a cake</u> and I take a piece of **the cake**.)

Je vois <u>un gâteau</u> et j'**en** prends une part. (I see <u>a cake,</u> and I take a piece **of it**.)

Je prends **quoi** ? (**What** do I take?)

<u>Une part du gâteau</u>. (<u>a piece of the cake</u>.)

PS: The pronoun "en" always comes between the subject and the verb.

The others are used directly without referring to a previous COD: "Me" (Me), "Te" (You), "Nous" (Us), "Vous" (You). For example:

- Il **m'**aime (He loves **me**.)
- Le prof **nous** pose quelques questions. (The teacher is asking **us** some questions.)

Exercise 1: Replace the COD with the correct pronoun in case of repetition.

1. Ma femme aime les fleurs, elle était contente de recevoir des fleurs aujourd'hui. (My wife loves

76

flowers, she was happy to receive flowers today.): _

_____

_____

2. Il reçoit un cadeau et ouvre le cadeau. (He receives a gift and opens the gift.): _____

_____

_____

3. J'ouvre le livre et commence à lire le livre. (I open a book and start reading the book.): _____

_____

_____

4. Ma mère m'a demandé de faire la vaisselle donc je fais la vaisselle. (Mom asked me to do the dishes so I'm doing the dishes.): _____

_____

_____

5. Les enfants sont avec moi donc je dépose les enfants à l'école. (The kids are with me so I drop off the kids at school.): _____

_____

_____

6. J'adore les fraises je mange des fraises tout le temps. (I love strawberries, I eat strawberries all the time.): _____

_____

_____

Exercise 2: Underline the COD pronouns

1. Mon père me porte jusqu'au lit. (My dad carries me to my bed.)
2. Le guide vous accompagnera à l'entrée. (The guide will accompany you at the entrance.)
3. Elle te regarde depuis sa fenêtre. (She's looking at you from her window.)
4. Ma sœur nous a perdus de vue. (My sister lost sight of us.)

Day 22: COI Pronouns

Lesson Reminder:

In French they're called "pronoms compléments indirectes" or "pronoms COI", let's take a look at them:

Some of them are used to replace a COI in a paragraph after it's been mentioned once before to avoid repetition: "Lui" (Him/Her), and "Leur" (Them). To figure out which item of the sentence they refer to, simply ask the questions "À qui ?/À quoi ?" or "De qui ?/De quoi ?"

For example:

Je parle à <u>mes parents</u> et je dis à **mes parents** que je sors. (I'm talking to <u>my parents,</u> and I tell **my parents** that I'm going out.)

Je parle à <u>mes parents</u> et je **leur** dis que je sors. (I'm talking to <u>my parents,</u> and I tell **them** that I'm going out.)

Je dis **à qui** que je sors ? (**Who** do I say I'm going out to?)

À <u>mes parents.</u> (To <u>my parents</u>.)

The pronoun "en" also replaces a previously

mentioned COI that comes after the preposition "de" to avoid repetition. In this case, "en" usually means "it/them". To figure out the function and which item of the sentence it refers to, simply ask the questions "De qui ?/De quoi ?".

For example:

Elle a <u>de mauvaises notes</u> mais elle se fout **des mauvaises notes**. (She has <u>bad grades,</u> but she doesn't care about **the bad grades**.)

Elle a <u>de mauvaises notes</u> mais elle s'**en** fout. (She has <u>bad grades,</u> but she doesn't care about **them**.)

Elle se fout **de quoi** ? (**What** doesn't she care **about**?)

<u>Des mauvaises notes</u>. (About <u>the bad grades</u>.)

The others are used directly without referring to a previous COI: "Me" (Me), "Te" (You), "Nous" (Us), and "Vous" (You). For example:

– Il **te** parle. (He's talking to **you**.)

– Elle pense beaucoup à **vous**. (She thinks of **you** a lot.)

Exercise 1: Replace the COI with the correct pronoun in case of repetition.

1. Ne prends pas mes affaires j'ai besoin de mes affaires. (Don't take my stuff, I need my stuff): ____

   _____

   _____

2. Ma copine aime beaucoup ses parents et obéit tout le temps à ses parents. (My friend loves her parents a lot and she always does what her parents say.): ___

   _____

   _____

3. J'ai parlé à ta mère, tu manques beaucoup à ta mère. (I spoke to your mom, your mom misses you a lot.): _____

   _____

4. Ce plat n'a pas assez de sel, il manque un peu de sel. (This dish doesn't have enough salt, it needs a bit more salt): _____

   _____

5. Éric est ton meilleur ami, tu devrais faire confiance à Éric. (Eric is your best friend, you should trust Eric.): _____

_____

6. La petite fille joue avec ses frères, elle fait peur à ses frères et rigole. (The little girl is playing with her brothers, she scares her brothers and laughs.):

_____

_____

Exercise 2: Underline the COI pronouns.

1. Je sais qu'elle te plait. (I know you like her.)
2. Mon ami nous a téléphonés. (my friend called us.).
3. Elle pense que ce livre vous appartient. (I think this book belongs to you.)
4. Ça me convient parfaitement, merci ! (I'm perfectly okay with that, thank you!)

Day 23: The Pronoun "Y"

Lesson Reminder:

CCL function: The pronoun "y" replaces a CCL that has been previously mentioned in the sentence to avoid repetition. In this case, "y" usually means "there/from there". To figure out the function and which item of the sentence it refers to, simply ask the question "Où ?" (where?).

Example:

Tu étais <u>à la bibliothèque</u> ? Oui, j'étais **à la bibliothèque**. (Were you <u>at the library</u>? Yes, I was **at the library**.)

Tu étais <u>à la bibliothèque</u> ? Oui, j'**y** étais. (Were you <u>at the library</u>? Yes, I was **there**.)

Où étais-tu ? (**Where** were you?)

<u>À la bibliothèque</u>. (<u>At the library</u>.)

COI function: The pronoun "y" replaces a previously mentioned COI that comes after the preposition "à" to avoid repetition. In this case, "y" usually means "it/of it/about it". To figure out the function and which item of the sentence it refers to, simply ask the questions "À qui/À quoi?".

Example:

J'ai vu <u>des choses bizarres</u> aujourd'hui, je pense encore **à ces choses bizarres**. (I saw <u>some weird things</u> today, I'm still thinking **about those weird things**.)

J'ai vu <u>des choses bizarres</u> aujourd'hui, j'**y** pense encore. (I saw some <u>weird things</u> today, I'm still thinking **about them**.)

À quoi je pense ? (**What** am I thinking **about**?)

<u>À ces choses bizarres</u>. (<u>About those weird things</u>.)

Exercise 1: Identify the functions of the pronouns "en" and "y" and underline the item of the sentence they're referring to.

1. Nous étions au cinéma hier soir, il y'avait un monde fou ! (We were at the cinema yesterday evening, there were so many people!): _____

84

2. Mes parents ont laissé mes frères avec moi donc je m'en occupe. (My parents left my brothers with me, so I'm taking care of them.): _____

3. Elle n'a pas lu tous les livres de Cate Tiernan, elle n'en connait que quelques uns. (She hasn't read all of Cate Tiernan's books, she only knows some of them.): _____

4. Mon frère avait de grands rêves, mais il y a renoncé pour prendre soin de nous. (My brother had big dreams, but he gave up on them to take care of us.): _____

5. Ce collier appartenait à sa grand-mère, elle y tient beaucoup. (This necklace belonged to her grandma, she's very attached to it.): _____

6. Mon ami adore le café, il en a bu trois verres aujourd'hui. (My friend really likes coffee, he's had three cups today.): _____

7. Tu as cherché dans le tiroir ? Ton écharpe y était la dernière fois que j'ai rangé. (Did you look in the drawer? Your scarf was there last time I cleaned up.): _____

8. Le réchauffement climatique est un vrai danger et vous vous en moquez ? (Global warming is a real threat, and you don't care about it?): _____

Exercise 2: Replace the repetition with the pronoun "y" and precise its function.

1. Elle est revenue de l'Italie, elle a passé une semaine en Italie. (She came back from Italy she spent a week in Italy.): _____

   _____

2. Mon fils passe beaucoup de temps avec League of Legends, il joue à League of Legends tous les jours. (My son spends a lot of time on League of Legends, he plays League of Legends everyday.):

   _____

   _____

3. Sa fille aime rester chez sa copine, elle a passé deux nuits chez sa copine. (His daughter likes to stay over at her friend's house, she spent two days at her friend's.): _____

   _____

4. On m'a proposée de faire un tour en Asie, je réfléchis toujours à faire un tour en Asie. (They offered me a tour in Asia, I'm still thinking about the tour in Asia.): _____

_____

Chapter VI: Possessive Pronouns & Adjectives

Day 24: Possessive Adjectives 1

Lesson Reminder:

"Mon" and "Ma": They both translate to "my", but "mon" is for something masculine, and "ma" is for something feminine. For example: C'est **mon** livre. (It's **my** book.); C'est **ma** place. (It's **my** place.)

"Ton" and "Ta": They both translate to "your", but "ton" is for something masculine, and "ta" is for something feminine. For example: C'est **ton** cahier. (It's **your** notebook.); C'est **ta** photo. (It's **your** photo.)

"Son" and "Sa": They translate to "his" and "her", but it doesn't depend on the person, it depends on <u>the thing</u> that belongs to the person, where "son" is for masculine things and "sa" is for feminine things. For example: <u>le bureau</u> de **Linda** (**Linda**'s <u>desk</u>) -> **Son**

bureau (**her** <u>desk</u>). Even though "Linda" is a feminine noun, we use "son" because "le bureau" is a masculine noun, unlike in English, where "his" and "her" refer to the person rather than the object.

PS: "mon", "ton", and "son" can be used to refer to feminine objects and nouns if they start with a vowel or an "H". For example: **Mon** amie Sarah. (**My** friend Sarah.)

"**Notre**": It translates to "our", it is gender-neutral, but it refers to singular objects that belong to several people. For example: **Notre** mère (**our** mother); Notre père (**our** father).

"**Votre**": It translates to "your" in plural form, it is gender-neutral, but it also refers to singular objects that belong to several people. For example: **Votre** sœur (**your** sister); **Votre** frère (**your** brother).

"Leur": It translates to "their", it is gender-neutral, but it refers to singular objects that belong to several people. For example: **Leur** tante (**their** aunt); **Leur** oncle (**their** uncle).

PS: Be careful not to confuse this "leur" with the COI pronoun; if the pronoun "leur" comes before a noun, it's a possessive pronoun. If it comes before a verb, it's a COI pronoun.

Exercise: Fill in the blanks with the correct possessive adjective.

1. Une famille : _____ famille (your [plural] family)
2. Une école : _____ école (our school)
3. Un sac : _____ sac (my bag)
4. Une poche : _____ poche (his pocket)
5. Une voiture : _____ voiture (their car)
6. Un jouet : _____ jouet (your toy).
7. Un chien : _____ chien (our dog)
8. Une maison : _____ maison (my house)

9. Un piano : _____ piano (her piano)

10. Un appartement : _____ appartement (their apartment)

11. Une tenue : _____ tenue (your outfit)

12. Un ami : _____ ami (your [plural] friend).

Day 25: Possessive Adjectives 2

Lesson Reminder:

"Mes": It translates to "my", but it is used for plural objects that belong to one person. It's gender-neutral. For example: **mes** écouteurs (**my** headphones); **mes** plantes (**my** plants).

"Tes": It translates to "your", but it is used for plural objects that belong to one person. It's gender-neutral. For example: **tes** stylos (**your** pens); **tes** photos (**your** photos).

"Ses": It translates to "his" or "her", but it's gender-neutral, and it is used for plural objects that belong to one person. For example: **ses** robes (**his/her** dresses); **ses** chats (**his/her** cats).

"Nos": It translates to "our" but it is used for plural objects that belong to several people, it's gender-neutral. For example: **nos** cousins (**our** cousins); **nos** rues (**our** streets).

"Vos": It translates to "your", but it is used for plural objects that belong to several people. It's gender-neutral. For example: **vos** costumes (**your** costumes); **vos** chemises (**your** shirts).

"Leurs": It translates to "their" but it is used for plural objects that belong to several people. It's gender-neutral. For example: **leurs** directeurs (**their** directors); **leurs** allergies (**their** allergies).

Exercise: Fill in the blanks using the correct possessive adjective.

1. Des animaux : _____ animaux (his/her animals)

2. Des idées : _____ idées (my ideas)

3. Des parents : _____ parents (your [plural] parents)

4. Des poupées : _____ poupées (your dolls)

5. Des dessins : _____ dessins (my drawings)

6. Des assiettes : _____ assiettes (their plates)

7. Des jeux-vidéos : _____ jeux-vidéos (our video games)

8. Des jupes : _____ jupes (his/her skirts)

9. Des rapports : _____ rapports (their reports)

10. Des notes : _____ notes (our grades)

11. Des examens : _____ examens (your exams)

12. Des fleurs : _____ fleurs (your (plural) flowers)

Day 26: Possessive Pronouns 1

Lesson Reminder:

We use this form of possessive pronouns to avoid repeating the name of the thing that we're talking about.

"le + mon" = "le mien": It translates to "mine"; it is only used with masculine nouns and objects. For example: C'est **ton livre**? Oui, c'est <u>le mien</u>. (Is this **your book**? Yes, it's <u>mine</u>.)

"la + ma" = "la mienne": It translates to "mine"; it is only used with feminine nouns and objects. For example: C'est **ta chaise**? Oui, c'est <u>la mienne</u>. (Is this **your chair**? Yes, it's <u>mine</u>.)

"le + ton" = "le tien": It translates to "yours"; it is only used with masculine nouns and objects. For example: C'est **ton cartable**? Non, c'est le <u>tien</u>. (Is this **your schoolbag**? No, it's <u>yours</u>.)

"la + ta" = "la tienne": It translates to "yours"; it is only used with feminine nouns and objects. For example: C'est **ta robe**? Non, c'est <u>la tienne</u>. (Is this **your dress**? No, it's <u>yours</u>.)

"le + son" = "le sien": It translates to "his" or "hers", it is only used with masculine nouns and objects. For example: C'est **ton sandwich**? Non, c'est <u>le sien</u>. (Is this **your sandwich**? No, it's <u>his</u>/<u>hers</u>.)

"le + sa" = "la sienne": It translates to "his" or "hers", it is only used with feminine nouns and objects. For example: C'est **sa montre**? Oui, c'est <u>la sienne</u>. (It this **his/her watch**? Yes, it's <u>his</u>/<u>hers</u>.)

"Le + notre" stays "le notre": It translates to "ours"; it is only used with singular masculine nouns and objects that belong to several people. For example: C'est **votre jardin**? Oui, C'est <u>le notre</u>. (Is this **your yard**? Yes, it's <u>ours</u>.)

Exercise: Fill in the blanks with the correct possessive pronoun.

1. Un article (an article): _____ (mine)

2. Un parfum (a perfume): _____ (his/hers)

3. Une brosse à dents (a toothbrush): _____ (yours)

4. Une épouse (a spouse): _____ (his/hers)

5. Un bouquet (a bouquet): _____ (yours)

6. Une décoration (a decoration): _____ (mine)

Day 27: Possessive Pronouns 2

Lesson Reminder:

"La + notre" stays "la notre": It translates to "ours"; it is only used with singular feminine nouns and objects that belong to several people. For example: C'est **votre maison**? Oui c'est <u>la notre.</u> (Is this **your house**? Yes, it's <u>ours.</u>)

"Le + votre" stays "le votre": It translates to "yours"; it is only used with singular masculine nouns and objects that belong to several people. For example: C'est **votre serveur** ? Non, c'est <u>le vôtre.</u> (Is this **your server**? No, it's <u>yours.</u>)

"La + votre" stays "la votre": It translates to "yours"; it is only used with singular feminine nouns and objects that belong to several people. For example: C'est **votre réservation** ? Non, c'est <u>la vôtre.</u> (Is this **your reservation**? No, it's <u>yours.</u>)

"Le + leur" stays "le leur": It translates to "theirs"; it is only used with singular masculine nouns and objects that belong to several people. For example: C'est **votre garage** ? Non, c'est <u>le leur.</u> (Is this **your garage**? No, it's <u>theirs.</u>)

"La + leur" stays "la leur": It translates to "theirs"; it is only used with singular feminine nouns and objects that belong to several people. For example: C'est **votre nièce** ? Non c'est <u>la leur.</u> (Is this **your niece**? No, she's <u>theirs.</u>)

Exercise: Fill in the blanks with the correct possessive pronoun.

1. Une machine à café (a coffee machine): _____ (theirs)

2. Un président (a president): _____ (ours)

3. Un trésor (a treasure): _____ (yours, plural)

4. Une cour (a courtyard): _____ (ours)

5. Un neveu (a nephew): _____ (theirs)

6. Une fête (a party): _____ (yours, plural)

Day 28: Possessive Pronouns 3

Lesson Reminder:

"Les + mes" = "les miens" or "les miennes": They both translate to "mine", but "les miens" is used with masculine objects, and "les miennes" is used with feminine ones. They both refer to several objects belonging to one person. For example:

- C'est **tes fils** ? Oui, c'est <u>les miens.</u> (Are these **your sons**? Yes, they're <u>mine.</u>)

- C'est tes filles ? Oui, c'est <u>les miennes.</u> (Are these **your daughters**? Yes, they're <u>mine.</u>)

"Les + tes" = "les tiens" or "les tiennes": They both translate to "yours", but "les tiens" is used with masculine objects, and "les tiennes" is used with feminine ones. They both refer to several objects belonging to one person. For example:

- C'est **mes colis** ? Oui, c'est <u>les tiens.</u> (Are these **my packages**? Yes, they're <u>yours.</u>)
- C'est **mes lunettes** ? Oui, c'est <u>les tiennes.</u> (Are these **my glasses**? Yes, they're <u>yours.</u>)

"Les + ses" = "les siens" or "les siennes": They both translate to "his" or "hers", but "les siens" is used with masculine objects, and "les siennes" is used with feminine ones. They both refer to several objects belonging to one person. For example:

- C'est **tes bracelets** ? Non, c'est <u>les siens.</u> (Are these **your bracelets** ? No, they're <u>his/hers.</u>)
- C'est **tes chaussures** ? Non, c'est <u>les siennes.</u> (Are these **your shoes**? No, they're <u>his/hers.</u>)

"Les + Nos" = "les nôtres": It translates to "ours",

it refers to several things belonging to several people, and it is gender-neutral. For example: C'est **vos téléphones** ? Oui, c'est <u>les nôtres.</u> (Are these **your phones**? Yes, they're <u>ours.</u>)

"Les + vos" = "les vôtres": It translates to "yours" in plural form, it refers to several things belonging to several people, and it is gender-neutral. For example: C'est **vos tapis** ? Non c'est <u>les vôtres.</u> (Are these **your carpets**? No, they're <u>yours.</u>)

"Les + leurs" stays "les leurs": It translates to "theirs", it refers to several things belonging to several people, and it is gender-neutral. For example: C'est **vos chambres** ? Non, c'est <u>les leurs.</u> (Are these **your rooms**? No, they're <u>theirs.</u>)

Exercise: Fill in the blanks with the correct possessive pronoun.

1. Des poissons (fish): _____ (ours)
2. Des sessions (sessions): _____ (mine)

3. Des compliments (compliments): _____ (yours)

4. Des devoirs (homework): _____ (his/hers)

5. Des manteaux (coats): _____ (theirs)

6. Des chances (chances): _____ (yours)

7. Des messages (messages): _____ (mine)

8. Des tatouages (tattoos): _____ (yours, plural)

9. Des aventures (adventures): _____ (his/hers).

Chapter VII: Demonstrative Pronouns And Adjectives

Day 29: Demonstrative Adjectives

Lesson Reminder:

"Ce": It translates to "this" but it's only used with masculine nouns and objects. For example: **ce** tapis (**this** carpet); **ce** cadre (**this** frame).

"Cet": It translates to "this", but it's only used with masculine nouns and objects that start with a vowel or an "H". For example: **cet** ouvrier (**this** employee); **cet** homme (**this** man).

"Cette": It also translates to "this", but it's only used with feminine nouns and objects. For example: **cette** lampe (**this** lamp); **cette** vie (**this** life).

"Ces": It translates to "these", it's gender-neutral and used just like in English. For example: **ces** arbres (**these** trees); **ces** métaphores (**these** metaphors).

Exercise 1: Fill in the blanks using the correct demonstrative adjective.

1. _____ espoir (hope)
2. _____ options (options)
3. _____ cristal (crystal)
4. _____ fourrure (fur)
5. _____ confiance (confidence)
6. _____ hommage (tribute)
7. _____ canaux (canals)
8. _____ lavage (washing)

Exercise 2: Transform the following demonstrative adjectives into the correct form.

1. Cette chanteuse (this singer): _____ chanteur
2. Ce comédien (this comedian): _____ comedienne
3. Ces motifs (these patterns): _____ motif
4. Cet auteur (this author): _____ auteurs
5. Cette admiratrice (this admirer): _____ admirateur
6. Ce chiffon (this cloth): _____ chiffons
7. Ces agriculteurs (these farmers): _____ agriculteur

8. Cet ennuyeux (this boring person): _____ ennuyeuse

Day 30: Demonstrative Pronouns

Lesson Reminder:

They are used to avoid repetition or to indicate a specific item out of many.

"Celui-là": It translates to "this one" but is used for masculine nouns and objects. For example: Tu veux quel gout ? Je veux **celui-là.** (Which flavor do you want? I want **this one.**)

"Celle-là": It translates to "this one" but is used for feminine nouns and objects. For example: Tu veux quelle robe ? Je veux **celle-là.** (Which dress do you want? I want **this one.**)

PS: "Celui-ci" and "celle-ci" are the exact same thing.

"Ceux-là": It translates to "these ones" but is used for masculine nouns and objects. For example: Tu as vu tous <u>ces films</u> ? Non, je n'ai vu que **ceux-là.** (Did you watch all <u>these movies</u>? No, I only watched **these ones.**)

"Celles-là": It translates to "these ones" but is used for feminine ones; they have the same role as the previous demonstrative pronouns. For example: Tu aimes <u>ces jupes</u>? Je préfère **celles-là.** (Do you like <u>these skirts</u>? I prefer **these ones.**)

PS: "Ceux-ci" and "celles-ci" are the exact same thing.

Exercise: Fill in the blanks using the correct demonstrative pronoun.

1. Une pâtisserie (a pastry): _____
2. Des balances (scales): _____
3. Des musiciens (musicians): _____

4. Un manoir (a manor): _____

5. Des chevaux (horses): _____

6. Une peinture (paint): _____

7. Un village (a town/village): _____

8. Des versions (versions): _____

Chapter VIII: Common Expressions & Homophones

Day 31: "Je Vais...", "Je Viens De...", And "En Train De..."

Lesson Reminder:

"Je vais...": This expression is used to indicate that the person saying it will take on the action that follows the preposition. It translates to "I will...". For example: **Je vais** terminer dans pas longtemps. (**I'll** be done in a bit); **Tu vas** y aller quand ? (When **will you** be going?)

"Je viens de...": This expression is used to indicate that the person saying it just finished doing an action. It translates to "I just finished..." or simply "I just...". For examples: **Je viens de** rentrer. (**I just** came back.); **Elle vient de** sortir. (**She just** went out.)

"En train de...": This expression is used to indicate that an action is taking happening for a long period of time, it doesn't have a translation to English, but the use of the "present continuous" tense gives the same effect. For examples: Je suis **en train de** dessiner. (I am drawing.); Nous sommes **entrain de** regarder un film. (we are watching a movie.)

A reminder of the conjugation of the verbs:

Je vais	Je viens	Je suis
Tu vas	Tu viens	Tu es
Il/Elle va	Il/Elle vient	Il/Elle est
Nous allons	Nous venons	Nous sommes
Vous allez	Vous venez	Vous êtes
Ils/Elles vont	Il/Elle viennent	Ils/Elles sont

Exercise: Fill in the blanks with the correct expression.

1. Je finis un livre. (I just finished a book.): _____ finir.

2. Mes parents m'accompagnent à la fête de l'école. (My parents will come with me to the school party.): Mes parents _____ m'accompagner.

3. Le guide annonce quelque chose d'important. (The guide is announcing something important.): Le guide _____ _____'annoncer.

4. Je conduis si tu te sens fatigue. (I will drive if you're tired.): _____ conduire.

5. Vous gaspillez votre argent. (You just wasted your money.): _____ gaspiller.

6. Ton frère et moi mettons la table. (Your brother and I just set the table.): Ton frère et moi _____ mettre.

Day 32: "Du Coup…" And "On Dirait…"

Lesson Reminder:

"**Du coup…**": This expression is mostly used in an informal speech. It translates to "and so…" or simply "so…" and it is used to indicate the result of a situation. For example: <u>Il pleuvait</u>, **du coup** <u>je suis pas sortie.</u> (<u>It was raining</u>, **so** <u>I didn't go out.</u>)

"**On dirait…**" or "**on dirait que…**": This

expression is used when comparing two things; it translates to "it looks like...". We use "on dirait..." before nouns and "on dirait que..." before verbs or when there is a verb in the sentence. For example:

- Ce chiot est tellement mignon, **on dirait** une peluche. (This puppy is so cute **it looks like** a stuffed toy.)
- Cette maison me fait peur, **on dirait qu'**elle est hantée. (This house scares me, **it looks like** it's haunted.)

Exercise: Fill in the blanks with the correct expression.

1. Tu es tellement beau, _____ un prince. (You're so handsome you look like a prince.)
2. Mon CV leur a plu, _____ ils m'ont embauchée. (They liked my resume, so they hired me.)
3. Les voisins d'à-côté crient sans arrêt, _____ ils se disputent. (The next-door neighbors keep yelling, it looks like they're fighting.)

4. Joseph a heurté sa cheville, _____ il boîte.
(Joseph hurt his ankle, so he's limping.)

5. Vous êtes passés devant nous sans nous saluer, _____ vous ne nous avez même pas reconnus.
(You passed in front of us without saying hello, it looked like you didn't even recognize us.)

6. La mer est tellement calme, _____ un tapis plat.
(The beach is so calm, it looks like a flat carpet.)

Day 33: Common Homophones

Lesson Reminder:

"à" and "a":

- **"à"** is a preposition that has multiple purposes we've seen before.
- **"a"** is the verb "avoir" (to have) conjugated with "il" and "elle".

"ça" and "sa":

- **"ça"** translates to "this" and it's a demonstrative adjective, but it is mostly used as a pronoun in sentences that don't have a real subject. For example: **ça** m'énerve (**it**'s annoying).

- **"sa"** is a possessive adjective we've seen before.

"ce" and "se":

- **"ce"** is a demonstrative adjective we've seen before, it always comes before nouns, except in sentences like "ce n'est pas vrai" (it's not true) or "ce n'est pas juste" (it's not fair).
- **"se"** is a personal pronoun we've seen before; it always comes before verbs.

"la" and "là"

- "la" is an article we've seen before, used before feminine nouns and objects.
- "là" means "here".

"mes" and "mais"

- **"mes"** is a possessive adjective we've seen before, used before plural nouns and objects.

- **"mais"** means "but".

"ces", "ses", and "sait/sais":

- **"ces"** is a demonstrative adjective we've seen before, used before plural nouns and objects.
- **"ses"** is a possessive adjective we've seen before, used before plural nouns and objects.
- **"sait" or "sais"** is the conjugation of the verb "savoir" (to know) with "il/elle" or "tu/je".

"ou" and "où":

- "ou" means "or".
- "où" means "where".

Exercise: Fill in the blanks with the correct homophone.

1. _____ me fait plaisir d'aider ma fille et _____ copine. (It's a pleasure to help my daughter and her friend.)

2. L'aéroport a perdu _____ valises, _____ ils disent qu'ils vont bientôt les récupérer. (The airport lost my luggage, but they say they'll soon get it back.)

3. _____! J'ai perdu _____ bague aux environs. (Here! I lost the ring in this area.)

4. Tu veux qu'on parte _____ cet été ? L'Indonésie _____ la Malaisie ? (Where do you want to go this summer? Indonesia or Malaysia?)

5. Mon ami _____ quelques soucis _____ la maison. (My friend has some problems at home.)

6. Je _____ que c'est cher, mais je veux toujours acheter _____ livres. (I know it's expensive, but I still want to buy these books.)

7. Elle _____ très bien que _____ notes seront mauvaises si elle ne révise pas. (She knows very well that her grades will be bad if she doesn't study.)

8. Ils _____ bagarrent pour avoir _____ téléphone soldé. (They're fighting each other to get that phone on sale.)

Chapter IX: Negative & Interrogative Forms

Day 34: Negative Form

Lesson Reminder:

There are many ways to form a negative sentence; let's take a look at them:

Using "ne... pas...": This form is the simplest and most common one, the "ne" comes before the verb, and the "pas" comes after. For example: Il fume. -> Il **ne** fume **pas.** (He smokes. -> He does**n't** smoke.)

Using "ne... jamais...": This form is simply translated to "never...". For example: J'y vais souvent. -> Je **n'**y vais **jamais.** (I go there often. -> I **never** go there.)

Using "ne... plus...": This form is used to indicate that someone has been doing something for a while, but they're not doing it anymore or to warn someone no to do something anymore. For example: Il obtient de bonnes notes. -> Il **n'**obtient **plus** de bonnes notes. (He gets good grades. -> He doesn**'t** get good grades **anymore**.)

Using "**ne... personne**" and "**ne... rien**": They roughly translate to "...anyone" and "...anything", they take the function of a COD. For example: Je **n'**entends **personne.** (I can**'t** hear **anyone.**); Tu **ne** vois **rien.** (You can**'t** see **anything.**)

Using "**personne ne...**" and "**rien ne...**": They roughly translate to "no one..." and "nothing...", they take the function of a subject. For example: **Personne** ne bouge. (**No one** is moving.); **Rien** n'est clair. (**Nothing** is clear.)

Using "**ne... ni... ni...**": This form cancels two (or more, with the addition of more "ni") things, it translates to "neither... nor...". For example: Je **n'**aime **ni** les bananes **ni** les pommes. (I **don't** like **neither** bananas **nor** apples.)

Exercise: Turn the following sentences into the correct negative form.

1. Tout ça va rentrer dans ta valise. (All this will fit inside your suitcase.): _____

    _____

    _____ ("rien ne...")

2. Mes parents ont visité Londres. (My parents visited London.): _____

    _____

    _____ ("ne... jamais...")

3. Nous voyons tout d'ici. (We can see everything from here.): _____

    _____

    _____ ("ne... rien...")

4. L'ouvrier est venu à l'heure. (The employee came on time.): _____

    _____

    _____ ("ne... pas...")

5. Tout le monde s'amuse. (Everyone is having fun):

    _____

_____

_____ ("personne ne...")

6. Je lis avant de dormir. (I read before I go to sleep.):

_____

_____

_____ ("ne... plus...")

7. Ma petite sœur aime les poupées et les petites voitures. (My little sister likes dolls and car toys.):

_____

_____

_____ ("ne... ni... ni")

8. Il inspire tout le monde avec ses discours. (He inspires everyone with his speeches.):

_____

_____

_____ ("ne... personne")

Day 35: Simple Interrogative Form

Lesson Reminder:

Using "est-ce que...": This is the simplest form of asking a question in French; it translates to "is...". For example: **Est-ce que** ta soupe est assez chaude ? (**Is your soup hot enough?**).

Switching places between the verb and the subject: This form is a bit tricky but easy once you get the hang of it. For example: **Vous voyez** les nuage. -> **Voyez-vous** les nuages ? (**You see** the clouds. -> **Do you see** the clouds?).

PS: When using this form with "il/elle", you must add a "t" between the pronoun and the verb unless the verb ends with a "t". For example: **Il habite** à Boston. -> **Habite-t-il** à Boston ? (**He lives** in Boston. -> **Does he live** in Boston?).

Exercise: Use the indicated interrogative form to turn the following sentences into questions.

1. Elle aime nager. (she likes swimming.): _____

    _____

    _____? (switching)

2. Le résultat des analyses médicales est sorti. (The medical tests result is out.): _____

_____

_____ ? (Est-ce que)

3. Tu es partie à l'école ce matin. (You went to school this morning.): _____

_____

_____? (switching)

4. Ça va dépendre de son arrivée. (It will depend on his arrival.): _____

_____

_____ ? (est-ce que)

5. Vous confirmez la réception de ce message. (You confirm receiving this message.): _____

_____

_____? (switching)

6. Nous déménageons bientôt. (We'll move out soon.):

_____

_____

_____? (Est-ce que)

Day 36: Interrogative Form Using Adverbs

Lesson Reminder:

"Que", "qu'…" or "quoi": They translate to "what". For example:

- **Que** lis-tu ? (**What** are you reading?)
- **Qu'est-ce que** vous faites ? (**What** are you doing?)
- Tu prépares **quoi**? (**What** are you preparing?)

"Qui": It translates to "who". For example: Tu parles **à qui** ? (**Who** are you talking to?)

"Quand": It translates to "when". For example: Il est parti **quand** ? (**When** did he leave?)

"Pourquoi": It translates to "why". For example: **Pourquoi** as-tu sali tes chaussures ? (**Why** did you dirty up your shoes?)

"Comment": It translates to "how". For example:

Comment t'as fait ça ? (**How** did you do that?)

"Où": It translates to "where". For example: **Où** sont-ils ? (**Where** are they?)

"Quel" and its derivatives: They translate to "which" or "what", they are mostly used to pick between two or more things.

– **"Quel"**: Used before masculine singular nouns and objects.

– **"Quelle"**: Used before feminine singular nouns and objects.

– **"Quels"**: Used before masculine plural nouns and objects.

– **"Quelles"**: Used before feminine plural nouns and objects.

"Quel" used after prepositions:

– **"À quel"**: It translates to "to which" or "to what".

– **"De quel"**: It translates to "of which" or "of what".

- **"Pour quel"**: It translates to "for which" or "for what".

- **"Sur quel"**: It translates to "on which" or "on what".

- **"Dans quel"**: It translates to "in which" or "on what".

Exercise: Use the correct adverb to ask questions about what's underlined.

1. Elles sont parties <u>en Turquie</u> hier. (They went to Turkey yesterday.): _____

   _____

2. On déjeune <u>à midi.</u> (We eat lunch at 12 pm.): _____

   _____

3. Vous allez mettre <u>ces robes.</u> (You're going to wear these dresses.): _____

   / _____

4. J'ai fait du retard <u>parce qu'il y'avait trop de circulation.</u> (I was late because there was too much traffic.): _____

   _____

5. Nous étions tous <u>souriants</u> en prenant la photo. (We were all smiley when taking the picture.): ____

   _____

6. <u>Peter</u> est venu avec moi. (Peter came with me.): __

   _____

Answers:

Chapter I: Pronunciation

Day 1: Letters S, C And G

First exercise	Second exercise	Third exercise
Un gosse : S	Du sucre: K	Des griffes : G
Ils lisent: Z	Le lycée: S	Agiter: J
Mon estomac: S	Un garçon: S	Un aveugle: G
Le magasin: Z	Un cri: K	Je nage: J
Une fusée: Z	Cette: S	Des algues: G
Tu essaies: S/mute	Convaincre: K/K	Une gorge: G/J
Un sosie: S/Z	Un accident: K/S	Un glaçage: G/J

Day 2: Letter E And Sounds "Qu" And "Gn"

Exercise 1		Exercise 2		Exercise 3	
La fête	e / mute	Une époque	k	Ignorer	nyo
Un retour	ea	Des quêtes	ke	La ligne	ny
Tu feras	ea	Quarante	ka	Témoignage	nya
Du thé	e	Quitter	ki	Une bagnole	nyo
Un poème	e / mute	Le traqueur	kea	Souligné	nye
Une tenue	ea / mute	Un cirque	k	Signification	nyi
L'église	e / mute	Manqué	ke	Espagnol	nyo
Devenir	ea / ea	Elle taquine	ki	Ma compagne	ny

Day 3: Sounds

Word	Sound	Sounds like	Word	Sound	Sounds like
Assez	"ez"	e (get)	Une cuisine	"ui"	ui
Un bateau	"eau"	o (Polly)	L'avion	"on"	on (only)
Épuiser	"ui"/"er"	ui (quick)/e	Des tiroirs	"oi"	wa (one)
L'ampoule	"am"/"ou"	ou (group)	Le mouton	"ou"/"on"	ou/on
Des nœuds	"œu"	ea (earn)	Seize	"ei"	e
Une fraise	"ai"	e	Un œuf	"œu"	ea
Beaucoup	"eau"/"ou"	o/ou	Le carnet	"et"	e

Chapter II: Genders, Plurals, And Their Articles

Day 4: Genders

Word	Gender	Word	Gender
Sortie	F	Voyage	M
Carnaval	M	Soir	M
Quartier	M	Fumée	F
Agence	F	Chevelure	F

Day 5: Plurals

Exercise 1		Exercise 2	
Oral	Oraux	Eaux	Eau
Joyau	Joyaux	Rails	Rail
Portail	Portails	Stylos	Stylo
Oiseau	Oiseaux	Neveux	Neveu
Flou	Flous	Chandails	Chandail
Nez	Nez	Clous	Clou
Canal	Canaux	Feuilles	Feuilles
Concours	Concours	Manteaux	Manteau

Day 6: Articles

Exercise 1		Exercise 2	
The cruelty	La cruauté	Un mal	Des maux
An advancement	Un avancement	Le pinceau	Des pinceaux
The opinion	L'opinion	L'épieu	Les épieux
The mirror	Le miroir	La souris	Les souris
A glow	Une lueur	Un iglou	Des iglous
(The) journalism	Le journalisme	Le camail	Les camails
(The) steel	L'acier	Une voix	Des voix
A revenge	Une vengeance	L'os	Les os

Day 7: Switching Genders

Exercise 1		Exercise 2		Exercise 3		
Prisonnier	Prisonnière	politicienne	politicien	Policier	M	Policière
Jaloux	Jalouse	Rêveuse	Rêveur	Spectatrice	F	Spectateur
Dépressif	Dépressive	Sorcière	Sorcier	Facultatif	M	Facultative
Végétarien	Végétarienne	Bouchère	Boucher	Chanceux	M	Chanceuse
Frimeur	Frimeuse	Audacieuse	Audacieux	Espionne	F	Espion
Lion	Lionne	Animatrice	Animateur	Menteur	M	Menteuse
Passager	Passagère	Sportive	Sportif	Chère	F	Cher
Conducteur	Conductrice	Chatonne	Chaton	Logisticienne	F	Logisticien

Chapter III: Adjectives And Prepositions

Day 8: Adjectives

Exercise 1			Exercise 2	
La soupe est chaude	F	S	Gentille	Gentilles
Le film est trop long	M	S	Douloureux	Douloureuses
Des stylos verts	M	P	Protectrices	Protecteur
Ces robes sont chères	F	P	Mauvais	Mauvaises
Une belle écriture	F	S	Craintifs	Craintive
Des rues lumineuses	F	P	Dernière	Derniers
Le restaurant est ouvert	M	S	Pluvieux	Pluvieuse
Je suis heureux	M	S	Légères	Léger

Exercise 3	
Il est adorable	A
Un endroit mystérieux	E
La pièce semble spacieuse	A
Des réunions importantes	E
Tu as l'air anxieuse	A
Un réponse fausse	E
Un voyage fatigant	E
Les dégâts sont considérables	A

Day 9: Prepositions Related To Time 1

1. Range ta chambre **quand** tu finis.
2. Mon vol est **à** 1h 30.
3. Tu dois être présent 30 minutes **avant** le début.
4. Va voir ta tante **après** le dîner.
5. Les heures de visite sont **de** 11h **à** 15h.
6. Le train arrive **dans** 15 minutes.
7. J'adore faire des randonnées **au** printemps.
8. Elles seront occupées **du** Dimanche **au** Jeudi.

Day 10: Prepositions Related To Time 2

1. Le magasin est ouvert **jusqu'à** 20h.
2. Tu peux me passer ton cahier **pendant** la récréation s'il te plaît ?
3. On part à Tokyo **en** été.
4. Ils sont mariés **depuis** 5 ans.
5. Je commence à travailler **à partir de** Lundi prochain.

6. La pièce est devenue silencieuse **dès que** le film a commencé.

7. Il reste à l'hôpital **jusqu'en** Décembre.

Day 11: Prepositions Related To Space 1

1. Mon hamster était **sous** le chapeau.

2. La Statue de la Liberté se trouve **à** New York.

3. Le parc est **près de** la plage.

4. Mon sac est **à côté de** tes affaires.

5. J'ai une belle veilleuse **au-dessus de** ma table de nuit.

6. Il y'a une librairie non **loin de** de notre école.

7. Il a mis tes clefs **sur** le bar.

8. En entrant dans le magasin, tu trouveras le riz **à gauche de** la section des pâtes.

9. Mon chien aime rester **au-dessus** du chauffage durant les journées froides.

Day 12: Prepositions Related De Space 2

1. Elle est **chez** la coiffeuse.

2. Tu dois passer **par** cette ruelle.

3. Nous allons **vers** la plage.

4. Il y'a une petite boutique de vêtements **derrière** ce marché.

5. L'Afrique se trouve **au-delà de** la Mer Méditerranée.

6. Il s'est installé **en** Chine.

7. Il y'a une petite exposition d'arts **en face de** la grande villa.

8. Les ingrédients sont **dans** le troisième tiroir.

9. Ils sont tous **en dehors de** la salle de cinéma.

10. Le petit garçon marche **devant** ses parents.

11. Nous regardons le film **à travers** ces lunettes 3D.

Day 13: Important Preposition 1

1. Ils ont besoin de plus de pailles **en** acier.

2. J'ai mis mon t-shirt dans la machine **à** laver.

3. Le gâteau **aux** fruits de ma tante est délicieux.

4. Le vieux est sauve **grâce au** docteur qui était dans les environs.

5. J'ai vu un petit renard **entre** les buissons.

6. Emmène ton petit frère **avec** toi au parc.

7. Il fait chaud, ne sortez pas **sans** bouteilles d'eau.

8. **Malgré** ce que tout le monde dit, tu dois continuer à te battre pour tes rêves.

Day 14: Important Prepositions 2

1. Mon frère a eu une promotion **pour** ses efforts.

2. Elle a aimé toutes les robes **sauf** la rouge.

3. Son visage est rempli **de** joie.

4. Je suis **contre** les résultats du vote.

5. Je vais faire le tour d'Europe **par** train.

6. Je ne te prendrai pas avec moi que **sauf si** tu me promets de bien te comporter.

Chapter IV: Object Complements And Circumstantial Complements

Day 15: COD and COS

1. On a fait <u>un cours intéressant</u> aujourd'hui : **COD**

2. J'ai perdu <u>mon chapeau</u> de <u>Noël</u> : **COD / COS**

3. Mon père a fait <u>un gâteau</u> pour <u>mon anniversaire</u> : **COD/COS**

4. Mon cousin a perdu <u>ses lunettes</u> : **COD**

5. Je mange <u>mon diner</u> : **COD**

6. Elle entend <u>son chien courir</u> en <u>ouvrant la porte</u> de son appartement : **COD / COS**

Day 16: COI

Exercise 1:

1. Prends soin de <u>ton petit frère</u> : **COI**

2. Ma mère a adoré <u>le cadeau</u> de <u>papa</u> ! **COD / COI**

3. Tu t'intéresses vraiment aux <u>arts</u> : **COI**

4. Elle a besoin du <u>médicament prescrit</u> : **COI**

5. Faites attentions aux <u>voitures</u> en traversant la route : **COI**

6. Nous tenons beaucoup à nos <u>chats</u> : **COI**

Exercise 2:

1. Nous <u>allons</u> à la plage : **VI**

2. <u>Passe</u> moi le couteau : **VTD**

3. Ça <u>dépend</u> du temps : **VTI**

4. <u>Ramenez</u> vos serviettes avec : **VTD**

5. Elle <u>est rentrée</u> de son voyage : **VTI**

6. Ils <u>habitent</u> à Toronto : **VI**

7. <u>Mettez</u> les chaises au fond : **VTD**

8. Mon père <u>se réveille</u> à 6h : **VI**

9. Tu <u>joues</u> à quoi ? **VTI**

Day 17: Circumstantial Complements

La maison était très calme <u>ce matin</u>	CCT
Les enfants jouent <u>bruyamment</u>	CCM
Nous dînons <u>à table</u>	CCL
Elle a géré l'événement <u>avec confiance</u> <u>hier</u>	CCM / CCT
Mon mari et moi partons <u>à Las Vegas</u> <u>en été</u>	CCL / CCT
Il marche <u>devant moi</u> <u>en toute timidité</u>	CCL / CCM
<u>L'autre jour</u> <u>au restaurant</u>, ton frère parlait <u>avec tristesse</u>	CCT / CCL / CCM

Chapter V: Personal Pronouns

Day 18: Subject Pronouns

1. **Il** a tout abandonné pour poursuivre sa passion.
2. Attention, **tu** vas tomber !
3. **Elles** sont endormies dans le salon.
4. **Je** pars chez ma grand-mère.
5. **Ils** chantent trop bien !
6. **Elle** enlève ses chaussures avant d'entrer.
7. **Nous** regardons un film triste.
8. **Vous** lisez quoi ?

Day 19: Tonic Pronouns

1. Je préfère la natation, et **toi** ?
2. Elles prennent toute la responsabilité sur **elles**.
3. Ton sac est devant **moi**.
4. **Elle**, elle vient de partir.
5. On passe la nuit chez **vous**.
6. Elle les attend avec **lui**.
7. J'ai acheté des glaces pour **nous** tous.
8. **Eux**, ils partent en Afrique.

Day 20: Reflected Pronouns

1. **Elle se** sont absentées.

2. **Tu te** trompes.

3. **Il se** lamente.

4. **Je me** méfie.

5. **Il s'**entre-tuent.

6. **Nous nous** rappelons.

7. **Elle se** fie à sa sœur.

8. **Vous vous** souciez trop.

Day 21: COD Pronouns

Exercise 1:

1. Ma femme aime les fleurs, elle était contente de recevoir des fleurs aujourd'hui -> Ma femme aime les fleurs, elle était contente d'**en** recevoir aujourd'hui.

2. Il reçoit un cadeau et ouvre le cadeau -> Il reçoit un cadeau et **l'**ouvre.

3. J'ouvre le livre et commence à lire le livre -> J'ouvre le livre et commence à **le** lire.
4. Ma mère m'a demandé de faire la vaisselle donc je fais la vaisselle -> Ma mère m'a demandé de faire la vaisselle donc je **la** fais.
5. Les enfants sont avec moi donc je dépose les enfants à l'école -> Les enfants sont avec moi donc je **les** dépose à l'école.
6. J'adore les fraises je mange des fraises tout le temps -> J'adore les fraises, j'**en** mange tout le temps.

Exercise 2:

1. Mon père <u>me</u> porte jusqu'au lit.
2. Le guide <u>vous</u> accompagnera à l'entrée.
3. Elle <u>te</u> regarde depuis sa fenêtre.
4. Ma sœur <u>nous</u> a perdus de vue.

Day 22: COI Pronouns

Exercise 1:

1. Ne prends pas mes affaires j'ai besoin de mes affaires -> Ne prends pas mes affaires j'**en** ai besoin.
2. Ma copine aime beaucoup ses parents et obéit tout le temps à ses parents -> Ma copine aime beaucoup ses parents et **leur** obéit tout le temps.
3. J'ai parlé à ta mère, tu manques beaucoup à ta mère -> J'ai parlé à ta mère, tu **lui** manques beaucoup.
4. Ce plat n'a pas assez de sel, il manque un peu de sel -> Ce plat n'a pas assez de sel, il **en** manque un peu.
5. Éric est ton meilleur ami, tu devrais faire confiance à Éric -> Éric est ton meilleur ami, tu devrais **lui** faire confiance.
6. La petite fille joue avec ses frères, elle fait peur à ses frères et rigole : -> La petite fille joue avec ses frères, elle **leur** fait peur et rigole.

Exercise 2:

1. Je sais qu'elle <u>te</u> plaît.
2. Mon ami <u>nous</u> a téléphonés.
3. Elle pense que ce livre <u>vous</u> appartient.
4. Ça <u>me</u> convient parfaitement, merci !

Day 23: The Pronoun "Y"

Exercise 1:

1. Nous étions <u>au cinéma</u> hier soir, il y'avait un monde fou ! **CCL**

2. Mes parents ont laissé <u>mes frères</u> avec moi donc je m'en occupe : **COI**

3. Elle n'a pas lu tous <u>les livres de Cate Tiernan</u>, elle n'en connait que quelques uns : **COD**

4. Mon frère avait <u>de grands rêves</u>, mais il y a renoncé pour prendre soin de nous : **COI**

5. <u>Ce collier</u> appartenait à sa grand-mère, elle y tient beaucoup : **COI**

6. Mon ami adore <u>le café</u>, il en a bu trois verres aujourd'hui : **COD**

7. Tu as cherché <u>dans le tiroir</u> ? Ton écharpe y était la dernière fois que j'ai rangé : **CCL**

8. <u>Le réchauffement climatique</u> est un vrai danger et vous vous en moquez ? **COI**

Exercise 2:

1. Elle est revenue de l'Italie, elle a passé une semaine en Italie -> Elle est revenue de l'Italie, elle y a passé une semaine.

2. Mon fils passe beaucoup de temps avec League of Legends, il joue à League of Legends tous les jours -> Mon fils passe beaucoup de temps avec League of Legends, il y joue tous les jours.

3. Sa fille aime rester chez sa copine, elle a passé deux nuits chez sa copine -> Sa fille aime rester chez sa copine, elle y passé deux nuits.

4. On m'a proposée de faire un tour en Asie, je réfléchis toujours à faire un tour en Asie -> On m'a proposée de faire un tour en Asie, j'y réfléchis toujours.

Chapter VI: Possessive Pronouns And Adjectives

Day 24: Possessive Adjectives 1

1. Une famille -> **Votre** famille.

2. Une école -> **Notre** école.

3. Un sac -> **Mon** sac.

4. Une poche -> **Sa** poche.

5. Une voiture -> **Leur** voiture.

6. Un jouet -> **Ton** jouet.

7. Un chien -> **Notre** chien.

8. Une maison -> **Ma** maison.

9. Un piano -> **Son** piano

10. Un appartement -> **Leur** appartement.

11. Une tenue -> **Ta** tenue.

12. Un ami -> **Votre** ami.

Day 25: Possessive Adjectives 2

1. Des animaux -> **Ses** animaux.

2. Des idées -> **Mes** idées.

3. Des parents -> **Vos** parents.

4. Des poupées -> **Tes** poupées.

5. Des dessins -> **Mes** dessins.

6. Des assiettes -> **Leurs** assiettes (their plates).

7. Des jeux-vidéos -> **Nos** jeux-vidéos.

8. Des jupes -> **Sa** jupes.

9. Des rapports -> **Leurs** rapports.

10. Des notes -> **Nos** notes.

11. Des examens -> **Tes** examens.

12. Des fleurs -> **Vos** fleurs.

Day 26: Possessive Pronouns 1

1. Un article -> **Le mien**.

2. Un parfum -> **Le sien**.

3. Une brosse à dents -> **La tienne**.

4. Une épouse -> **La sienne**.

5. Un bouquet -> **Le tien**.

6. Une décoration -> **La mienne**.

Day 27: Possessive Pronouns 2

1. Une machine à café -> **La leur**.

2. Un président -> **Le nôtre**.

3. Un trésor -> **Le vôtre**.

4. Une cour -> **La nôtre**.

5. Un neveu -> **Le leur**.

6. Une fête -> **La vôtre**.

Day 28: Possessive Pronouns 3

1. Des poissons -> **Les nôtres**.

2. Des sessions -> **Les miennes**.

3. Des compliments -> **Les tiens**.

4. Des devoirs -> **Les siens**.

5. Des manteaux -> **Les leurs**.

6. Des chances -> **Les tiennes**.

7. Des messages -> **Les miens**.

8. Des tatouages -> **Les vôtres**.

9. Des aventures -> **Les siennes**.

Chapter VII: Demonstrative Pronouns And Adjectives

Day 29: Demonstrative Adjectives

Exercise 1

1. **Cet** espoir.

2. **Ces** options.

3. **Ce** cristal.

4. **Cette** fourrure.

5. **Cette** confiance.

6. **Cet** hommage.

7. **Ces** canaux.

8. **Ce** lavage.

Exercise 2:

1. Cette chanteuse -> **Ce** chanteur.

2. Ce comédien -> **Cette** comédienne.

3. Ces motifs -> **Ce** motif.

4. Cet auteur -> **Ces** auteurs.

5. Cette admiratrice -> **Cet** admirateur.

6. Ce chiffon -> **Ces** chiffons.

7. Ces agriculteurs -> **Cet** agriculteur.

8. Cet ennuyeux -> **Cette** ennuyeuse.

Day 30: Demonstrative Pronouns

1. Une pâtisserie -> **Celle-là**.

2. Des balances -> **Celles-là**.

3. Des musiciens -> **Ceux-là**.

4. Un manoir -> **Celui-là**.

5. Des chevaux -> **Ceux-là**

6. Une peinture -> **Celle-là**.

7. Un village -> **Celui-là**.

8. Des versions -> **Celles-là**.

Chapter VIII: Common Expressions And Homophones

Day 31: "Je Vais…", "Je Viens De…" And "En Train De…"

1. Je finis un livre -> **Je viens de** finir un livre.

2. Mes parents m'accompagnent à la fête de l'école -> Mes parents **vont** m'accompagner.

3. Le guide annonce quelque chose d'important -> Le guide **est en train d**'annoncer.

4. Je conduis si tu te sens fatigue -> **Je vais** conduire.

5. Vous gaspillez votre argent -> **Vous venez de** gaspiller.

6. Ton frère et moi mettons la table -> Ton frère et moi **Venons de** mettre.

Day 32: "Du Coup…" And "On Dirait…"

1. Tu es tellement beau, **on dirait** un prince.

2. Mon CV leur a plu, **du coup** ils m'ont embauchée.

3. Les voisins d'à-côté crient sans arrêt, **on dirait qu'**ils se disputant.

4. Joseph a heurté sa cheville, **du coup** il boîte.

5. Vous êtes passés devant nous sans nous saluer, **on dirait que** vous ne nous avez même pas reconnus.

6. La mer est tellement calme, **on dirait** un tapis plat.

Day 33: Common Homophones

1. Ça me fait plaisir d'aider ma fille et **sa** copine.

2. L'aéroport a perdu **mes** valises, **mais** ils disent qu'ils vont bientôt les récupérer.

3. **Là** ! J'ai perdu **la** bague aux environs.

4. Tu veux qu'on parte **où** cet été ? L'Indonésie **ou** la Malaisie ?

5. Mon ami **a** quelques soucis **à** la maison.

6. Je **sais** que c'est cher, mais je veux toujours acheter **ces** livres.

7. Elle **sait** très bien que **ses** notes seront mauvaises si elle ne révise pas.

8. Ils **se** bagarrent pour avoir **ce** téléphone soldé.

Chapter IX: Negative And Interrogative Form

Day 34: Negative Form

1. Tout ça va rentrer dans ta valise -> **Rien ne** va rentrer dans ta valise.

2. Mes parents ont visité Londres -> Mes parents **n'**ont **jamais** visité Londres.

3. Nous voyons tout d'ici -> Nous **ne** voyons **rien** d'ici.

4. L'ouvrier est venu à l'heure -> L'ouvrier **n'**est **pas** venu à l'heure.

5. Tout le monde s'amuse -> **Personne ne** s'amuse.

6. Je lis avant de dormir -> Je **ne** lis **plus** avant de dormir.

7. Ma petite sœur aime les poupées et les petites voitures -> Ma petite sœur **n'**aime **ni** les poupées **ni** les petites voitures.

8. Il inspire tout le monde avec ses discours -> Il **n'**inspire **personne** avec ses discours.

Day 35: Simple Interrogative Form

1. Elle aime nager -> **Aime-t-elle** nager ?

2. Le résultat des analyses médicales est sorti -> **Est-ce que** le résultat des analyses médicales est sorti ?

3. Tu es partie à l'école ce matin -> **Es-tu** partie à l'école ce matin ?

4. Ça va dépendre de son arrivée -> **Est-ce** que ça va dépendre de son arrivée ?

5. Vous confirmez la réception de ce message -> **Confirmez-vous** la réception de ce message ?

6. Nous déménageons bientôt -> **Est-ce que** nous déménageons bientôt ?

Day 36: Interrogative Form Using Adverbs

1. Elles sont parties <u>en Turquie</u> hier -> Elles sont parties **où** hier ?

2. On déjeune <u>à midi</u> -> On déjeune **quand** ?

3. Vous allez mettre <u>ces robes</u> -> **Qu'**allez-vous mettre ? / Vous allez mettre **quoi** ?

4. J'ai fait du retard <u>parce qu'il y'avait trop de circulation</u> -> **Pourquoi** ai-je fait du retard ?

5. Nous étions tous <u>souriants</u> en prenant la photo ->

   Comment étions-nous en prégnant la photo ?

6. <u>Peter</u> est venu avec moi -> **Qui** est venu avec moi ?

Conclusion

Now that we have all the lessons fully explained and the exercises fully understood, it is time for us to leave the learning process up to you.

No one is perfect at something right from the start. You have to be okay with being a beginner to fully appreciate the journey of learning a new language and discovering it.

As Elizabeth Gilbert said in her book Big Magic: "Done is better than good [...], so if you can just complete something –merely complete it- you're already miles ahead of the pack right there."

Allow yourself imperfection but practice hard, and you WILL see great results.

References

1. Used to search for words: www.listedesmots.net

2. Used to find rules of masculine and feminine nouns and objects: www.bonjourdefrance.com

3. Used to find rules of going from singular to plural form: www.francaisfacile.com

4. Used to find rules of going from masculine to feminine form: www.francaisfacile.com

5. Used to find the list of prepositions: www.francais.lingolia.com

Disclaimer

The information contained in this book and its components, is meant to serve as a comprehensive collection of strategies that the author of this book has done research about. Summaries, strategies, tips and tricks are only recommendations by the author, and reading this book will not guarantee that one's results will exactly mirror the author's results.

The author of this book has made all reasonable efforts to provide current and accurate information for the readers of this book. The author and its associates will not be held liable for any unintentional errors or omissions that may be found.

The material in the book may include information by third-parties. Third-party materials comprise of opinions expressed by their owners. As such, the author of this book does not assume responsibility or liability for any third-party material or opinions.

from the author.

Made in the USA
Coppell, TX
08 September 2020